American Tweetheart

@TeaPainUSA

ISBN-13: 978-1975631888

ISBN-10: 1975631889

DEDICATION

Tea Pain wants to thank all the followers on the Tea Pain Train, the finest crew on Twitter! Whooo! Whooo!

Tea Pain would also like to thank George Takei, Malcolm Nance and Rachel Dratch for their kind comments on the back cover.

CONTENTS

1. GROWIN' UP TEA PAIN

 Tea Pain
@TeaPainUSA

There's too much love and truth in Tea Pain for just one person.

Before we get started, there's somethin' you need to know about ol' Tea Pain. First of all, he talks and tweets different than most folks. Some folks call it talkin' in the "third person." Tea Pain's talked this way since he was a little critter. Coincidentally, there's three reasons why he talks this way:

1. Tea Pain learned early on that you should respect your parents. "Honor thy father and mother, and your days shall be long upon the earth." - Exodus 20:12. Tea's mama and daddy always called him "Tea Pain" or "Tea," so Tea Pain did the same thing outta respect. When the kids at school made fun, Mama would say, "Tea Pain, there is too much love and truth in you for just one person." That was all Tea Pain needed to hear.

2. God exists in three persons: the Father, the Son and the Holy Ghost. Reckon if three persons is good enough for the good Lord, it's good enough for ol' Tea Pain.

3. Tea Pain noticed that sports stars, professional wrestlers and rap artists often speak in the third person, and they always have lotsa women and money, so there's that.

There's another thing you'll notice in this book. Tea Pain's had a number of careers: a wrestler, reporter, preacher and rapper. Tea Pain made his livin' for a while remixin' hit songs with political messages. Tea Pain's gonna share one of his tasty remixes at the end of each chapter. Hope they're dope!

Tea Pain
@TeaPainUSA

Tea Pain was born Thomas Elmer Addison Pain on July 4th, 1976 in Cooter Creek Arkansas.

Tea Pain was born, but he don't remember much about it, so this part of the story is gonna be pretty much hearsay.

Tea Pain came three weeks early and caught his folks off guard. He ended up bein' born on July the 4th, 1976. Guess ol' Tea Pain insisted on bein' born on the same birthday as the greatest nation on the face of the Earth. Tea's folks loved America dearly and always flew a big American flag on the front porch on patriotic holidays. But this holiday, labor came on Tea's mama so quick there wasn't time to get to the hospital.

Fortunately ol' Doc Harbuck, the local vet, lived nearby. He came runnin' and helped Tea's mama bring ol' Tea Pain into this world kickin' and screamin'. Tea's folks were mighty embarrassed there wasn't even a swaddlin' blanket in the house, so Tea's daddy went out on the porch, pulled down Old Glory and wrapped baby Tea in it. Something about that flag had a calmin' effect, and Little Tea quieted right down. Truth be told, Tea Pain's always felt mighty comforted by the good ol' Stars and Stripes.

Tea Pain
@TeaPainUSA

Replying to @ahd20422566 and 2 others

Tea Pain was born in Cooter Creek, AR, Home of the famous "Mullet Festival." Know what mullets are?

Cooter Creek ain't a bad place to be from. It's in North Central Arkansas in the eastern half of Fartlett County and is known for its famous "Mullet Festival." Contrary to what you're thinkin', "mullet" has nothin' to do with the hairstyle, though plenty of folks in Cooter Creek still sport that look. "Mullet" is a type of schoolin' baitfish, easily confused with minners. First weekend of every August, folks catch all the mullets they can get a net on and fry 'em up like hushpuppies. Mighty tasty! Combine that with our annual Mule Jump, and you got a weekend full of family entertainment.

Now in these parts there's two class of folks: Flatlanders and Ridge Runners. Livin' in Cooter Creek made us Flatlanders, but every Flatlander quietly envied folks that lived up in the hills. Tea's daddy promised that if we ever came into a little money, we'd move. Like every good Arkansan, it was his lifelong dream to live high up on a mountain top.

Funny thing about life: sometimes you get what you wish for, but it don't come in the container you expected. Tea's daddy was a mighty good man and, like every man full of decency and virtue, he had a tiny crack here and there. Daddy Pain liked to have a drop or two of whiskey every now and then but was too proud to buy the store-bought stuff, so he made his own.

Not to brag, but Tea's daddy was the finest distiller in all of Fartlett County. Folks would come from miles around to sample what

Daddy rendered. But you never knew if one of them folks might be from the gubment, so Tea's daddy never cooked at the house. He was a smart feller. He always cooked up in this hollered out place in the bluffs of Cooter Creek. Daddy knew if he used regular wood, the smoke would draw them revenuers like a politician to a super PAC, so he used propane. He liked that it provided even heat and, even better, was 100% smokeless.

Daddy used to use this propane burner he'd bought on sale up at the Harrison Walmart for 24 bucks. Turns out this burner got recalled for a safety issue with the regulator, but news like that seldom makes it to these parts. One day Daddy was about to fire up a fresh batch when, "Whoom!" Folks say you could see the fireball as far away as Jasper.

We were able to put Daddy out pretty quick, so he only had minor burns and some scuffs here and there. An attorney from over in Jasper heard about it and showed up one day with a big leather briefcase promisin' that millions of dollars would come rollin' in if Daddy was to file a "personal injury lawsuit" - minus his third, of course.

At first Daddy's pride wouldn't let him have nothin' to do with it. It was too much like charity, and Daddy never took charity. But when Mama assured him it wouldn't hurt nothin' to let the lawyer talk to the propane burner company, he gave in.

Even though Daddy had the propane burner folks dead-to-rights, there was some loophole about the burner bein' used to commit a felony or some silly thing like that. To make everything quietly go away, the propane burner company wrote Daddy a $10,000 check, provided he sign a nine page non-disclosure agreement first. With that money, Tea's daddy was finally able to make his dream of bein' a real Ridge Runner come true. We was able to buy a tiny native stone house built in 1932 in a little neighborhood named Gizzard Ridge, which would become Tea Pain's home to this day.

Tea Pain
@TeaPainUSA

@TovarRasputin @JadedByPolitics Gizzard Ridge is the
county seat of Fartlett county.
11:05 PM - Oct 1, 2014

Fartlett county, in Tea's humble opinion, is the paradise of the
United States. It's got pretty mountains, clean rivers and streams,
good huntin' and some of the nicest folks you'll meet this side of
heaven.

Gizzard Ridge is the county seat of Fartlett County. Fartlett County
was named after the famous Southern Civil War guerrilla fighter,
Colonel Richard "Dick" Fartlett. Fartlett trained his men to move
through the woods without breakin' a stick or makin' a sound, just
like the Cherokee. They were known to sneak up on ya from
behind and take you by total surprise. Union soldiers all agreed that
ol' Colonel Dick and his men were "silent but deadly." They were
always spoken of in hushed and reverent tones; nary a Union
soldier would dare make a Dick or a Fartlett joke.

There's a bit more to this story. Fartlett County ain't found on
maps anymore. About 20 years ago, historians discovered that
Colonel Fartlett used an unsavory process for extractin'
information from Union prisoners of war. The scholars didn't go
into too much detail except that his process involved a series of
blankets, a hot day and a technique called a "Dutch Oven." Not
wantin' to be tainted by the stink of another scandal, the state
legislature voted unanimously to merge Fartlett county into
Newton county. With the stroke of a pen, the legend of Colonel
Fartlett passed into the winds of history.

Tea Pain
@TeaPainUSA

@lkatrell The hat is ol' Tea Pain's trademark. That would be like taking Michael Jackson's glove or Rand Paul's toupee.
9:14 PM - Aug 15, 2014

Remember how Tea's folks swaddled him in the American flag when he was born? Turns out Tea got so attached to that flag that he toted it around like a security blanket. When Tea's daddy tried to take it from him, Tea would fuss and cry for hours and hours, finally wearin' his daddy down till he surrendered and gave it back. Little Tea would crawl all over the house with that flag in tow. You need to understand, Tea's folks were mighty patriotic and feared this might be seen as desecratin' the symbol of our great nation, so Mama had a real good idea.

One night while little Tea was asleep, Mama snuck the blanket from him and took it back to her sewin' room. She worked all night; cuttin' and a-sewin' to beat the band. When Tea Pain woke the next mornin', he reached instinctively for Old Glory. When she was nowhere to be found, Tea started screamin' like the panthers roamin' the Cooter Creek bottoms at night.

Mama eased into Tea's room with something under her apron. This was Mama's signal that Tea Pain had a special surprise comin', but he wasn't sure what.

Out from her apron, Mama Pain revealed the thing that would change Tea Pain's life forever. She had turned Tea Pain's security blanket into the most beautiful hat he'd ever seen! Tea Pain quieted down instantly. He would have cried tears of joy, but since he was a little feller and lacked the emotional development, he just grinned.

Mama put the hat on Little Tea and held him in front of the mirror. Little Tea beamed with pride beyond his years. Since then, Tea Pain's only taken that hat off twice. Once when his daddy went

6

to his heavenly reward, and again when his dear mama went to rest in the arms of Brother Jesus.

Tea Pain had to retire the original hat years ago. He keeps it in a little oak box he made special for it. Whenever he misses his folks, he pulls it out, and it makes him feel better. Tea Pain was a mighty lucky feller to have such good folks that loved him and loved America.

Tea Pain
@TeaPainUSA

Tea Pain's got two of the finest huntin' dogs in Fartlett county.
1:35 PM - Jan 14, 2016

Tea's Two Huntin' Dogs

"BEN"   "GHAZI"

It wouldn't be braggin' to say that Tea Pain has the two best huntin' dogs in the county. Tea bred 'em back when he was in the Tea Party, so he called 'em "Ben" and "Ghazi."

Tea Pain took 'em to all the Tea Party picnics. All Tea Pain had to do was call 'em to get the fun started. Every time Tea Pain would yell "Ben!" "Ghazi!" the Tea Party folks would get all worked up and start carryin' on! Them was some good times.

Tea Pain
@TeaPainUSA

@Kris_SacreBleu Tea's the chairman of the
Gizzard Ridge Teddy Cruz 2016 headquarters!
11:23 PM - Sep 25, 2014

Back in 2012, ol' Ted Cruz came outta nowhere as the leader of the
Tea Party. Lookin' back, it's kinda funny that a bunch of Anglo-
Saxon Tea Partiers anointed a Canadian-born Cuban whose father
was a Communist to lead the charge against brown-skinned folks.
But that's the good thing about politics: it don't have to make sense
- you just have to vote.

Tea Pain don't do nothin' half-way, and ol' Teddy couldn't have
had a bigger fan or a more zealous spokesperson than ol' Tea Pain.
That is, until October of 2013.

You see, the crown jewel of North Arkansas is the Buffalo
National Riverway. There ain't a prettier or better river anywhere
for a good old-fashioned float trip. Folks come from six states to
float its cool, clear spring-fed waters, driftin' carefree along with
the current beneath 100 foot limestone bluffs. You might even
catch a glimpse of a herd of elk if you're lucky. It is truly a work of
God's own hand.

About this same time, Ted Cruz was jockeyin' his way to the head of the 2016 pack of hopefuls vyin' to run for President. He saw his openin' in the battle royale that was shapin' up over the budget fight in Washington, D.C. Ted said this was the Tea Party's chance to fight for "smaller gubment" and to show that dictator Obama that he wasn't king no more!

We all cheered Teddy on as he led that filibuster all night, preachin' about the constitution and readin' Dr. Seuss's "Green Eggs and Ham." Nothin' would show those stuck-up Washington Liberals we were a bonafide political movement like a grown man readin' from a children's book!

Teddy managed to charm a bunch of his feller Republicans into joinin' him in shuttin' down the gubment, and the fight was on!

Folks, the old sayin' that "all politics is local" is a truthful statement if there ever was one, cause that weekend Tea Pain and his posse packed up the canoes in the back of our pickups and lit out to float and party on the Buffalo. Little did we realize that shuttin' down the gubment also meant shuttin' down our national parks. To our surprise, when we arrived all the gates were shut, and we were turned away by military-lookin' security in black Chevy Tahoes sportin' 9 millimeter side arms. For just a moment, we all felt like criminals for wantin' to enjoy' the National Riverway we always took for granted.

That night, Tea Pain had the strangest dream. He woke up in a cold sweat and was overcome by the Holy Ghost to write it all down. What came from that anointed fever dream was Tea Pain's first "political epiphany." Tea stared in disbelief at the words that just a moment ago danced uncontrollably from his fountain pen:

The Temptation of Tea Pain

In a vision Ted Cruz took me up on a big tall mountain
And showed me all the Koch brothers money flowin'like a fountain
So just like any normal feller would Tea jumped in and started drinkin'
While Ted just stood there, smilin' and winkin'
The ground started shakin' and at my feet were all my fellow citizens
Drinkin' dirty water, breathin' dirty air, barely makin' a living
Women forced to bear their attackers babies, nevermind they was the victim
And none of the faithful had rights less they was white, male and Christian
Ted lit a cigar with a hundred dollar bill and said "Tea"
"This fountain can be yores if you will bow down before me."
And in that instant that sweet water turned bitter in my mouth
"Never", Tea cried, as Tea turned and spit it out
"It's written in the scripture "Love thy neighbor as yoreselves"
"Get behind me Teddy, cause we see yore the devil!"

It's like the Good Lord himself wrote those words just for Tea Pain, in rhymin' verse, no less. In an instant, Tea Pain's newly opened mind could extrapolate his current political platform to its logical, yet absurd conclusion. Tea Pain recoiled instantly when he realized he'd been votin' against his own best interests all these years.

Tea Pain is not one for inaction, so he instinctively did two things:

1. He tweeted the following:

 **Tea Pain**
@TeaPainUSA

First. Effective immediately, Tea Pain's resigning his position as grand chairman of the "Gizzard Ridge Committee to Elect Ted Cruz in 2016."
2:04 PM - Nov 6, 2014

2. Then he called a press conference.

Tea Pain Press Release

@TeaPainUSA

Ol' Tea Pain's been a member of the Tea Party way back even before Bush was President. In the past six years, we've watched my party go down a road that don't make ol' Tea Pain proud anymore. Sadly, the Tea Party has become a requiem for racists, a haven for haters, and an sanctuary for the sanctimonious. As a matter of fact, lib'rals and moderate Republicans have been kinder to Tea Pain than his own party. Today Tea Pain's announcing that he will answer the call and become the leader of the new "Progressive Wing" of the Tea Party.

And the rest, as they say, is Twitter history.

2. SEPARATION OF CHURCH AND HATE

Tea Pain
@TeaPainUSA

Wouldn't America be a better place if Conservatives believed in the separation of Church and Hate?

Tea Pain's been blessed with a good life full of interestin' careers, but his most rewardin' one was his first: the ministry. Tea Pain was raised Southern Baptist and went to church every Sunday and every Wednesday night at the Gizzard Ridge Baptist Church.

Our pastor was a right likable feller named G.O. Fishen and, true to his name, he was a born "Fisher of Men." He was a big, loud feller with a big smile and a big voice. Tea Pain swore he was the livin' embodiment of the Apostle John... that is, if the Apostle John drank a little. Unfortunately, he was also a "Fisher of Fish," and after a Saturday night visitin' with Homer and Bud Felix at their still, he forgot what day it was and chose to salve his mornin' hangover on the lake communin' with the Good Lord and the crappies.

That same Sunday morning we was all singin' and praisin' the Lord, when it came time for Brother Fishen's sermon. People started gettin' antsy cause they realized the good pastor was nowhere to be found. That's when Tea Pain heard his first callin' at only 11 years old.

Amongst the confusion and overcome by the Spirit, Tea Pain grabbed his Bible and quietly walked up front. The pulpit was too tall, so Tea opened his Bible, stood on the steps of the altar and began to preach about how Jesus loves everybody and how He died for us and how He wants everybody to love everybody else. The Lord laid a mighty message on young Tea Pain's heart that mornin'. Tea can't remember a word he said cause the Holy Ghost had ahold of him, but it musta been a powerful annointin'. Just about everybody came down front to get saved, some for their fourth or fifth time.

The church deacons were a little vexed at the idea of a youngster preachin' the Gospel to a buncha grownups. That is, until they tallied up the offerin' plates and found the church tripled its normal contribution. After that, they encouraged the regular pastor to go fishin' anytime he liked.

Tea Pain
@TeaPainUSA

Ever since they lost the civil war, Conservatives keep inventin' new wars hopin' maybe they can win just one. #WarOnWhites #WarOnChristmas

One thing Tea Pain never understood was folks complainin' about how the gubment wants to "take away our religious freedoms." They were always lamentin' about how America was strayin' from its "Christian principles" and that some kinda "war" was bein' waged against Christianity. Just name something, and chances were good there was a war against it. There was a "War Against Marriage," a "War Against Christianity" and Fox's annual "War on Christmas." One year it got so bad, Tea Pain was afraid to put up his Christmas lights for fear of a drive-by shootin'.

Tea Pain went to Memphis once when he was a young man. It was like dyin' and goin' to Heaven cause you couldn't sail a pie pan in that town without hittin' a barbecue joint. And the only thing Memphis has more of than barbecue joints is churches. Tea soon found himself sittin' in Dixie's Pit Bar-B-Q, eatin' a jumbo chopped pork sandwich with some delicious baked beans. As he dined on some of the best barbecue he ever put in his mouth, he noticed the Presbyterian church across the street, the Baptist church on the corner and the Methodist church next door. If there really was a war against Christianity, Christianity was definitely winnin'.

Tea Pain
@TeaPainUSA

The Tea Party believes in the separation of Church and Reality.

2:00 PM - Dec 3, 2015

💬 6   🔁 104   ♡ 107

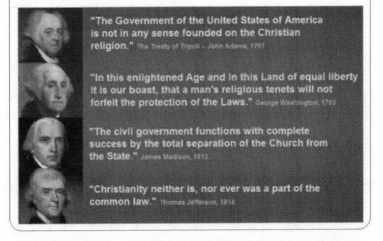

"The Government of the United States of America is not in any sense founded on the Christian religion." The Treaty of Tripoli – John Adams, 1797

"In this enlightened Age and in this Land of equal liberty it is our boast, that a man's religious tenets will not forfeit the protection of the Laws." George Washington, 1793

"The civil government functions with complete success by the total separation of the Church from the State." James Madison, 1813

"Christianity neither is, nor ever was a part of the common law." Thomas Jefferson, 1814

Another thing puzzles Tea Pain. A lotta folks in Gizzard Ridge argue that America is a "Christian Nation" and that all our laws should be "Christian." This takes Tea Pain back to a Sunday mornin' bible study years ago. We was studyin' the Book of Leviticus and got to the part where it says, "You shall not lie with a man as with a woman; it is an abomination." - Lev. 18:22

Sister Mildred, who specialized in the "Thou Shalt Nots," was quick to jump in.

"God's word is clear! We need to stop them Liberals from givin' our country away to the gays! We need to ban the gays before they take over!"

"The Bible says we need to stone 'em. Just sayin'!", echoed Brother Donald. "Them Liberals is always pushin' that 'church and state' nonsense on us. That's a bunch of bull hockey; there oughta be a law!"

Tea Pain was taken aback by how quickly this Bible study had taken such an un-Christian turn.

"Brothers and sisters," said Tea Pain, slowly risin' to his feet. "Remember just a few weeks ago when we read Leviticus 11 about them dietary laws? Sister Mildred, are you ready to give up shrimp and catfish?"

Every Sunday for the past eight years, after the closin' prayer Sister Mildred made a beeline to the Catfish Hole up in Harrison, loadin' up on fried catfish, shrimp and them finger lickin' hush puppies. (Tea's gonna give you a little tip. Try dippin' your hushpuppies in melted butter. You might die young, but you'll die happy.)

"W-w-well now, that's different," protested Sister Mildred. "We ain't the Israelites!"

"And what about you, Brother Donald?" asked Tea Pain. "You ready to give up the Skid Mark's scrumptious pork nachos and watchin' Sunday afternoon football? We don't wanna encourage ol' Brett Favre to sin tossin' that abominable pigskin around, now do we?"

Stavin' off what appeared to be a mini-stroke, Brother Donald gathered his composure and framed his counter-attack.

"We ain't under the Law of Moses no more," he thundered, as if he was Matlock himself. "We's under a new law."

Brother Donald's words settled on the congregation like a soft rain, soothin' some of the folks that feared they might have to give up shrimp, pork and the NFL all in the same day. Tea Pain flipped to the book of Mark. "Then let's just see what the 'New Law' says, shall we?"

"Anyone who divorces his wife and marries another woman commits adultery against her. And if she divorces her husband and marries another man, she commits adultery." - Mark 10:11-12

At the readin' of this verse, most of the room got jumpier than a hound dog on hot pavement. Gizzard Ridge ain't much different than anywhere else. The only thing more popular here than marriage is gettin' outta your previous one.

After this little incident, the Sunday School Committee held an emergency session and decided to stop studyin' Leviticus and switch to a less controversial topic… like the book of Revelation.

Tea Pain
@TeaPainUSA

Conservative Christianity has become less about learnin' to love your fellow man and more about learnin' which ones to hate.

10:14 AM - Dec 28, 2015

💬 86   🔁 1,077   ♡ 1,217

Remember Jesus's beautiful story of the Good Samaritan that helped the wounded man on the road when his own countrymen ignored him? The real importance of that story is lost on most folks here in America.

The Samaritans and the Jews were bitter enemies since the times of Jewish captivity by the Babylonians. To the Jews, the Samaritans were heretics - worse than the Gentiles - because they were keepers of the Torah, yet didn't foller it the way the Jews thought proper. They worshipped the same God and had the same basic laws, only the Samaritans had a different Holy Place than Jerusalem. Funny how folks feud the hardest with others that have so much in common with themselves.

The way Tea Pain sees it, this is just like Christians and Muslims today. They both worship the same God. They both sprang from Abraham. Ninety percent of their laws and teachings are virtually identical. Tea Pain bets if Jesus were preachin' today, the Samaritan in his story would have most likely been a Muslim and the Jew would have been a Christian.

Conservative Christians seem to miss Jesus's simple message every time: the good Lord wants us to love our neighbors, even though we might not see eye-to-eye with them on every tenet of religion or facet of philosophy. Funny thing with these Twitter Christians - you could substitute the Bible with an AR-15 manual, and they'd never know the difference.

- - -

White Christian

I'm voting for a White Christian
Just like the ones we used to know
Just like Ronald Reagan and old Todd Akin
Old men with flesh tones white as snow

I'm voting for a White Christian
To take away all women's rights
May your gays not marry for life
And may all yore Christian men be white

3. THE TEA PARTY'S OVER

 **Tea Pain**
@TeaPainUSA

A Liberal says "we need more friends."
A Conservative says "we need more enemies."
Tea Party says "shoot'em all and let God sort'em out."

Tea Pain's always been a Liberal, but he didn't always know it. It just so happens that before he figured it out, he was a member of the Tea Party, not so much for the politics but mainly because it had the word "party" in it. Tea Pain's always up for a party!

Lotsa folks think the Tea Party started in 2008 after Obama got elected, but that ain't entirely true. They've been around in different forms and by different names for years. You may have known 'em better as "rednecks," "yahoos" or "peckerwoods." But it wasn't till them Liberals elected a black president that they decided to get 'em a new name and a new flag.

> **Tea Pain**
> @TeaPainUSA
>
> In Gizzard Ridge, the Tea Party meets in the Baptist Church Sunday night at 7:00 pm. KKK meets at 8:00. Same folks go to both. #OpKKK #tcot

Back in the day, Tea Pain never missed a Tea Party meetin', mainly cause they served these delicious little oatmeal raisin cookies. Tea Pain could eat like fifty of 'em. During the meetings, folks would mainly spend their time talkin' about how Obama was like Hitler... that is, if Hitler had loved gays and blacks and Mexicans and wanted to make sure everybody had health insurance.

The real trick was to stay sharp, cause it was hard to tell when the Tea Party meetin' was over and the KKK meetin' started. The same folks were at both meetings, and they seemed to talk about the same stuff. Maybe these Tea Party fellers had just met some bad apples, cause Tea Pain worked for a while at the Tyson chicken plant over in Berryville with plenty of Mexicans and black folks, and they all treated Tea Pain really good, and we got along just fine.

> **Tea Pain**
> @TeaPainUSA
>
> Conservatives want smaller gub'ment for the same reasons bank robbers want fewer security cameras. #TeaBomb

Have you ever wondered why poor folks livin' on food stamps and other gubment assistance would care about "oppressive EPA clean water regulations?" What kind of silly fool votes against clean water? The same kind of silly fool that was told that since Obama is for clean water, it must be wrong.

It's works something like this: Cyanide Clyde owns a chemical factory on the Osage River. Havin' to properly dispose of his poisonous chemicals is cuttin' into his 60 million dollar annual profit. Downstream Dave lives on the Osage in a trailer park about 50 miles away. Clyde donates a hundred large every two years to his local Tea Party rep's campaign. The rep goes on TV and tells Downstream Dave that Hillary is a horrible crook, a murderer and drowns little kittens. Her emails are worse than 9/11 and Dave needs to oppose everything she stands for or all of America will soon be wearin' matchin' pantsuits. Dave loves America and hated what happened on 9/11, so he votes for Clyde's bought-and-paid-for Tea Party pony.

Six months later, President Trump eases the EPA clean water regulations, and Cyanide Clyde can now dump his toxic chemicals directly in the river. Downstream Dave notices one morning that his urine is significantly more phosphorescent than normal. He goes to the doctor but finds out Medicaid in his state was also cut by the same rep he voted for, and now he has no healthcare.

It's not all bad news for Dave, though. Now he can die happy knowin' that somewhere a chemical plant owner is havin' a bangin' coke party with Russian hookers on his new corporate jet.

Tea Pain
@TeaPainUSA
Q: What has a 100 legs and 14 teeth?
A: A Tea Party rally.

Did you know that the toothbrush was invented in Arkansas? If it was invented anywhere else, it would have been called a "teeth brush."

Tea Pain
@TeaPainUSA

Tea Party and ISIS are fightin' to see who overthrows the US gub'ment first. The Tea Party just happens to have the home-field advantage.

Remember when the Tea Party wanted to go to D.C. with their shootin' irons and take over the government? They called it "patriotism," but when ISIS proposes doin' the same thing, they call it "terrorism." Funny thing, they never talked about overthrowin' anything till that black feller got elected.

Once upon a time, the Tea Party dreamed of waltzin' into our nation's capital with their AR-15s and their pocket Constitutions they'd been meanin' to read since 2008 and arrest that dictator Obama, put him on trial, then hang him for the treasonous scoundrel he was. The Tea Party weren't exactly what you would call "original thinkers," so they labeled their little soiree "Operation American Spring" after the uprisin' in the Arab world. Tea Pain was so impressed by their little shin-dig, he wrote one of his first raps about it.

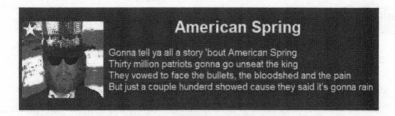

American Spring

Gonna tell ya all a story 'bout American Spring
Thirty million patriots gonna go unseat the king
They vowed to face the bullets, the bloodshed and the pain
But just a couple hunderd showed cause they said it's gonna rain

"Operation American Spring" showed what 30 million Tea Party patriots could do when they put their hearts and minds to it. Turnout estimates went as high as 400 people, but it looked closer to 275. They say there were more vendors there than actual protesters. When it was all over, they coulda went and ate in the same booth at Denny's.

Operation American Spring

Tea Pain
@TeaPainUSA

@HavanaTed You go brother Teddy! Thanks for takin' time from yore 5 week vacation to complain 'bout Obama playin' all that golf!

Teddy Cruz is the kind of lyin' scoundrel that gives garden-variety lyin' scoundrels a bad name. He's the kind of politician that could reach into your pocket, steal your cash, keys and credit cards, then claim it was your hand in there all along. He'd quickly pivot and preach you a sermon about how the Bible says it's wrong for you to have your hand in your pants pleasurin' yourself in the first place. He'd then immediately launch an email campaign and raise money off your self-abuse.

Tea Pain @TeaPainUSA · 17 Jun 2016
President Obama was just "stupid" enough to beat you and McCain by **192 electoral votes.** @SarahPalinUSA

> **Sarah Palin** ✔ @SarahPalinUSA
> OBAMA IS A SPECIAL KIND OF STUPID
>
> Enough is enough, Mr. President. There's no "due respect" due you after...
> fb.me/4EcSmqn9N

💬 59   ↻ 302   ♡ 529   �ⅼⅼ

If they ever erect a "Church of the Politically Irrelevant," Sarah Palin will be its founder and patron saint. Sarah Palin callin' somebody "stupid" is like Sarah Palin callin' somebody a "quitter" or a "hillbilly." Notice how nobody ever asked to see her college transcripts?

Tea Pain
@TeaPainUSA

The real reason Conservatives wanna protect the Constitution is because without it, Obama could beat them a 3rd and 4th time. #tcot

Remember how Republicans didn't care two shucks about the Constitution while white folks lived in the White House? They were passin' out our civil liberties like party favors when ol' Dubya asked 'em to. They never blinked an eye when Ronnie Reagan wrote executive orders faster than a meter maid on quota day.

Then along came Obama. Republicans discovered that old dusty relic would serve nicely as the foundation of their subliminal racist agenda to hold the first black president in check. Behold! The birth of the "Constitutional Conservatives!" Turns out the Tea Party was just as good at interpreting the Constitution as they were understanding the Bible, since they never spent any time readin' either one.

24

Remember how much trouble Nicholas Cage went through to steal the Declaration of Independence? If he'd just waited till Trump got elected, he could have bought it and the Constitution both for 50 cents at a White House garage sale.

Moral of this story: all Presidents are created equal, but White Presidents are created more equal than others.

Tea Pain
@TeaPainUSA

Tea Party Conservatives claim Obama can't nominate another #SCOTUS Justice because he's already served 3/5ths of his final term.

When Justice Scalia passed away, you could hear Republicans swallerin' their tongues at the possibility of President Obama appointin' another Liberal justice to the highest court in the land. First, a black feller in the White House? Then a second term, and now another appointment? Equality is a great concept and all, but this was just way too much.

Then Mitch McConnell remembered a law he just made up that black presidents can't appoint a justice in their last year in office. Republicans weren't 100% sure that was in the Constitution, but since it would require them to actually read it, they decided to just quietly go along.

Tea Pain
@TeaPainUSA

If Obama was really a dictator, the Tea Party would be in 4x4 cages, instead of on social media callin' Obama a dictator.

Obama turned out to be the weakest dictator in American history. Time and time again he failed to declare martial law, suspend elections or name himself "President for Life." Turns out this lawless dictator was done in by the one thing no one could have anticipated: constitutional term limits.

The Tea Party emerged victorious in their battle against Emperor Obama. Thanks to their tireless efforts postin' InfoWars memes on Facebook and Twitter, they bravely held Obama to only two terms!

Tea Pain
@TeaPainUSA

Tea Party nut balls keep sayin' Obama is just like Hitler, even though Obama's black, ends wars, and helps folks afford health insurance.

Tea Pain was most tickled when right-wing nutballs compared President Obama to Adolf Hitler. Actually, when you stop and think about it, politics today is the art of comparin' your opponents to Nazis before they return the favor.

The funniest moment might have been when Dr. Ben Carson compared America to Nazi Germany. Only a successful, rich, black doctor running for president could see the true parallels to Hitler... with the exception, of course, of Hitler not allowing minorities education, wealth or access to public office.

Tea Pain
@TeaPainUSA

Tea Party Thinkin': Obama is responsible when gas prices are high, but Frackin' is responsible when gas prices are low. #TeaBomb

Poor Obama could never catch any Tea Party love, even though his economy brought America back from financial ruin. The DOW was around 8,000 when he took office and near 20k when he left, but no Tea Partier would acknowledge a job well done. As a matter of fact, the millions of jobs created under his watch were all "the wrong kind," and the low gas prices were actually hurtin' the economy," though they never told us why.

On cue, the party that was 99.5% white proclaimed the Obama administration as the "darkest" period in American economics. Then Trump got elected, and all of a sudden the same "horrible economic indicators" were signs of a thrivin', boomin' white hot economy! The economic blackness had abated and the white, er, light had returned.

Tea Pain
@TeaPainUSA

Remember when the Tea Party was all over Twitter claimin' Exec Orders were un-Constitutional? They musta all got raptured.

7:11 PM - Jan 27, 2017   ◯ 121   ⟲ 2,126   ♡ 3,539

Tea Pain
@TeaPainUSA

Why ain't the Tea Party speakin' out about how Exec Orders are 'unconstitutional' like they did with the black president...oh...never mind.

1:27 AM - Jan 25, 2017   ◯ 114   ⟲ 2,583   ♡ 3,934

Don't get Tea Pain started on executive orders. In 2007, folks that would later join the Tea Party didn't even know what an executive order was, but by the time Obama was inaugurated, they were experts on the topic and convinced the Antichrist would usher in the end times via executive order. Executive orders are the "instruments of dictators" and "wholly unconstitutional," cried the unwashed and unholy patriots wavin' their yeller snake flags and wearin' their pointy hats.

Executive Orders by President

39	Jimmy Carter	320
40	Ronald Reagan	381
41	George H. W. Bush	166
42	Bill Clinton	364
43	George W. Bush	291
44	Barack Obama	276

Funny thing, when these same folks was a little younger, they voted for a feller named Ronnie Reagan. Turns out Reagan loved executive orders! As a matter of fact, Reagan loved 'em so much that, on average, he cranked one out every eight days!

This leaves us with a mystery. Why would the Tea Party, a group that is 99.5% white, not have a problem when a white president cranked out EOs like candy from a Pez dispenser, but get all bent outta shape when a black feller used 'em? Hmmm. Now what could it be?

Tea Pain
@TeaPainUSA

Looks like the Tea Party thinks "Political Correctness"
means havin' to spell the N-Word correctly when spray-
paintin' it on overpasses.

If you dropped Tea Pain out of a helicopter into a political rally, he
could tell you in five seconds if it was a Tea Party rally or not. He
wouldn't have to look for the yeller "Don't Tread On Me" flags or
scan for the predominant skin color of the participants. All he'd
have to do is check for the spellin' on the protest signs.

Tea Pain @TeaPainUSA · 21 Apr 2016
Wonder how many states this **Tea Party** nut ball thinks he can vote in? ->
@Sluggod54 <-

 ChattyGranddaddy @sluggod54 · Feb 13
@GOP Republicans had better delay ANY of Obama's Supreme Court choices
until after 1/20/17! I will not vote for any GOP senator that won't!

Tea Partiers love to try to make you believe they really care about
the Constitution. They fancy themselves "Constitutional scholars"
cause they read the second half of the Second Amendment like 400
times. This little feller is one of those "scholars." He threatened
every Republican senator to straighten up, or they wouldn't have
his vote. This Constitutional savant don't even understand that you
can only vote for one senator at a time in your own state.

Have you noticed how the Tea Party seems to have almost
disappeared? Remember how they chided Democrats as bein'
nothin' more than an Obama-cult? Now those same "patriots"
follow Donald Trump around like a lost puppy, cheerin' every
executive order and retweetin' every misspelled tweet like it's
Shakespeare. Since the black feller is no longer in the White House,
the facade of the "constitutional conservative" is no longer of use.
The Tea Party is alive and well and thrivin' under a new name: *The
Alt-Right*.

- - -

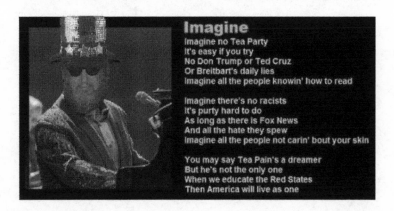

Imagine
Imagine no Tea Party
It's easy if you try
No Don Trump or Ted Cruz
Or Breitbart's daily lies
Imagine all the people knowin' how to read

Imagine there's no racists
It's purty hard to do
As long as there is Fox News
And all the hate they spew
Imagine all the people not carin' 'bout your skin

You may say Tea Pain's a dreamer
But he's not the only one
When we educate the Red States
Then America will live as one

4. RACISM AND THE ALT-RIGHT

Tea Pain
@TeaPainUSA

JFK: "Better to light a candle, than curse the darkness."

Alt-right: "Better to light a cross, then curse the dark ones."
4:43 PM - Oct 29, 2016

💬 34   🔁 373   ♡ 870

Tea Pain ain't known for sugar-coatin' stuff, and he ain't about to start now. Tea would love to tell you that we've outgrown racism in this country and we's on the path to total enlightenment, but that just ain't so. Despite Civil Rights and the election of our first black president, racism never went away - it just went underground. Racists is just like locusts. They don't die; they just lay there and wait.

All it took to unleash the latest plague on America was the Lord of the Flies himself, Donald Trump.

Tea Pain
@TeaPainUSA

Ignorant racists shout their racism from the rooftops. Clever racists quietly remove the voice and the rights of minorities.

11:44 AM - Feb 16, 2017

💬 31   🔁 707   ♡ 1,307

While Twitter has got more right-wing racists than Chris Brown has restrainin' orders, the real racists run for political office. They don't yell and scream vile racial obscenities; they make laws. Why oppress one brown-skinned feller, when you can oppress all of 'em at once?

Tea Pain
@TeaPainUSA

Giuliani blames "inner cities" for voter fraud. "Inner city" is the Alt-right's new n-word.

10:50 AM - Oct 16, 2016

💬 59   🔁 626   ♡ 943

The "smart" racist never utters the "n-word." He paints with a more colorful pallet of hate. Instead of spewin' hate like, "lazy black folks on food stamps," he uses phrases like "an inner-city culture that doesn't value work."

Trump ran as the "Law and Order" candidate, and the white supremacists lapped it up like free beer on Friday night. When you hear "Law and Order," you don't think of the FBI comin' down hard on white collar Wall Streeters or staffin' up the SEC to take down hedge-fund pirates. Nope. "Law and Order" was simply racial code for crackin' down on minority crime in the inner cities.

"Travel Bans" and "Stop and Frisk" were just two more forms of racial/religious profilin' designed to oppress Muslims and black folks and keep 'em under control. Notice how "illegal alien" never refers to Russian sex-workers snuck into America to service high-dollar executives, but to the lowly Mexican that picks our fruit and cuts our grass.

Tea Pain
@TeaPainUSA

Skin-heads have the thinnest skin.#BasketOfDeplorables
11:23 AM - Sep 10, 2016

💬 42　🔁 594　♡ 1,161

The Alt-Righties are always rippin' on Liberals, callin' them "sissies," "cucks" and "effeminate," but then they turn around and declare that they live in fear of these "violent savage lefties!" Ain't that a hoot?

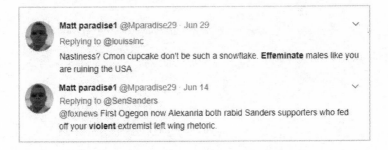

Matt paradise1 @Mparadise29 · Jun 29
Replying to @louissinc
Nastiness? Cmon cupcake don't be such a snowflake. **Effeminate** males like you are ruining the USA

Matt paradise1 @Mparadise29 · Jun 14
Replying to @SenSanders
@foxnews First Ogegon now Alexanria both rabid Sanders supporters who fed off your **violent** extremist left wing rhetoric.

Take ol' Matthew here. He can't make up his mind from one minute to the next. One day he's callin' liberal men "effeminate snowflakes." The next, he's tremblin' in his jack-boots in fear of their "violent extremism." Funny how these same rugged individualists that brought us "cucks," "pc police," "libtards" and "snowflakes" are now the cowerin' victims of the "rabid left."

Mike Cernovich 🔲 ⬤ @Cernovich · 2 Dec 2016
Fake news editors with a track record of covering up **pedophile** scandals oppose #Pizzagate. Makes you think.

 Mike Cernovich 🔲 ⬤ @Cernovich · 9 Dec 2016   ⌄
The Daily Beast, owned by Chelsea Clinton, is calling me a "neo-Nazi." Libel and fake news. Maybe I'll **sue** them.

Then there's the new breed of thin-skinned little Trump flakes like Mikey Cernovich. He stands behind the First Amendment to spread debunked foolishness like #pizzagate, an Alt-Right nutball story that the Clintons and their campaign manager, John Podesta, were runnin' an international pedophile operation out of the basement of a D.C. pizzeria. Problem is, the eatery in question don't even have a basement. One feller got arrested for believin' Mikey's little tale. Seein' himself as a one-man Alt-Right Justice League, he brought an assault rifle into the joint and almost got a lotta innocent folks killed.

Even though Cernovich is a foamin'-at-the-mouth mouthpiece of the Alt-Right movement, when the Daily Beast published an opinion piece suggestin' he was a "neo-Nazi," he did what all great defenders of free speech do: threatened to sue.

 2nd Republic @1776_Redux · 2 Aug 2016
Replying to @TeaPainUSA
I don't make idle threats son. If I promise **legal action**, it happens, and it happens when the defendant least expects it.

Tea Pain's lost count of how many times he's troll-rolled one of these chest-thumpin', First Amendment flingin', fire-breathin' Trump trolls, only to watch 'em turn around and threaten to sue because Tea Pain embarrassed 'em and hurt their feelings. Three guesses as to how many of these vanguards of freedom have actually sued? (Hint: zero)

Tea Pain
@TeaPainUSA

The Tea Party is why black Presidents can't have nice things. #tcot #pjnet #teaparty #ccot
1:31 PM - Sep 16, 2015

Kid Kebmod the Cool
@sluggoD54

Replying to @revteapain
@revteapain thedailybeast.com/articles/2015/... America is great for Obama! Free Jet to spew plenty Co2! Free phone vacations maids chefs etc...

The election of President Obama in 2008 heralded a huge comeback for public racism in America, and with it came the double-standard for presidents. Every round of golf was announced on Fox News - anything to make President Obama look "lazy." Plus any of the normal perks that came with the position were suddenly viewed with a jaundiced eye.

Take little Sluggo here. He was racism's "comeback kid," the poster child for the Tea Party's not-so-coded racism. How dare Obama have a "free phone" and take a vacation? Shouldn't he have to clean the White House himself? And other people actually prepare his meals for him? What a lazy freeloader!

If he had simply called him the "n-word," at least it would have been honest. Instead, a catalog of racist code emerged. "He's not like us." "President Obama don't understand the American experience," and "He's a secret Muslim."

Speakin' of racist code, check out Sluggo's screen name: "Kid Kebmod the Cool". Seems harmless enough, don't it? The original name of the KKK was the "Ku Klux Clan." Note the "KKC" initials in his name. A number of trolls used this racist code online until the Tea Pain Train exposed them, and many were forced to change it, includin' little Sluggo.

(As a side note to long-time Twitter users, "Sluggo" was later caught promotin' neo-Nazi propaganda from *Stormfront* and other white supremacist websites. His account is currently locked by Twitter.)

Tea Pain
@TeaPainUSA

Never has so many white folks labored to have their own health insurance taken away only because it was given to them by a black man.

1:32 PM - Jun 10, 2017

💬 873   🔁 15,717   ♡ 33,952

This may be one of the craziest things Tea Pain has ever seen in his whole life. Twenty million folks got insurance under Obamacare that never had it before - many of them Republicans - yet they couldn't wait to vote for Trump in hopes it would be repealed. Who would vote to take away their own insurance? What was different about this insurance? As of the writin' of this book, poor Republicans are clamorin' for a TrumpCare plan that will most likely double, even triple their premiums while lowerin' their coverage and make their deductibles sky-rocket. Tea Pain's always gonna tell you the truth, and he ain't gonna stop now. They want TrumpCare because it's the *white* thing to do!

The Trump candidacy gave hardcore racists legitimacy again. No longer seekin' solace in the dark and dreary corners of the Twitter-net, they came out in a white hot rage, so to speak. Leadin' the pack was this ol' scudder, "Raging Rob." Tea Pain lost track of how many times Rob had been banned from Twitter, only to open another account. Rob spent equal amounts of time praisin' the Lord and hatin' on black folks, just like Jesus did.

Tea Pain
@TeaPainUSA

God is strictly #ProLife, provided you don't ask the Philistines, Hittites, Amelikites or Canaanites #tcot #ccot #ProChoice.

John Mavry had been Deacon of the Gizzard Ridge Baptist Church since Tea Pain was a little critter. You know how there's always some folks at church every time the doors are open? Well, Deacon Mavry was the feller that opened the doors. He was dutiful to a fault, but he never smiled. If Christians are supposed to "bear fruits of the Spirit," brother Mavry was the least fruity feller you ever met. He was a man of few words - that is, until you came to his pet subject in Sunday School.

Over the years we studied pretty much the whole Bible, includin' the Old Testament, which was clearly Deacon Mavry's favorite. On one Sunday in particular, we was studyin' 1st Samuel, and we came to the passage where King Saul was told to "go and strike Amalek and utterly destroy all that he has, and do not spare him; but put to death both man and woman, child and infant, ox and sheep, camel and donkey.'"

Brother Mavry, who hadn't said ten words since Christmas, was suddenly John the Baptist. He started by explainin' about how Noah's son, Ham, was cursed when he "looked upon his father's nakedness." Although the Bible says nothin' on the matter, Brother Mavry's sources assured him that Ham, his son Canaan and all their descendants were cursed by God... turnin' their skin **black**. The Amalekites were, coincidentally, also descendants of Ham and, accordin' to brother Mavry, all shared the same pigmentation affliction. Tea Pain actually saw a gleam in the Deacon's eye as he lectured us on the "real reason" God said to destroy this race of folks in 1st Samuel.

Now there's a key piece of the story you ain't been told yet. Deacon Mavry was also a regular at the Knights of the Ku Klux Klan meetin' that met the first Sunday of every month in the church basement.

Then a couple years back, Deacon Mavry got mighty sick. Turns out his heart was failin' him. He got on a transplant list, and the whole church prayed regularly for him. Just as it appeared time for Brother Mavry to go to his reward, our prayers were answered, and the good brother got a new heart. Soon his health returned, and he was back to his regular post as a shepherd of the flock.

One Sunday we had some visitors down from Harrison, and they brought with them a mighty interestin' rumor. Turns out Brother Mavry's heart donor was a black feller! This is the only time anyone could remember brother John havin' to leave a service early. Guess some folks handle good news differently than others.

It was probably six months later when we were studyin' Deuteronomy and came upon the part where the Israelites

38

encountered the Canaanites - more of Ham's progeny. The teacher paused, knowing full well that Deacon Mavry would step in and school us further on his favorite topic. Instead, he just sat there studyin' his fingernails.

Over the next few years, folks saw a change come over the good deacon. He would greet folks with a smile and shake their hand. Some folks claim they even heard him laugh out loud once. It was also rumored he no longer attended the "not-so-secret" meetings in the basement. Reckon he had a true "change of heart."

Now, at this part of the story, you're surely askin' yourselves how anyone knew about the identity of the heart donor, since these lists are highly confidential. The next time the visitors from Harrison showed up, they were given the third degree by Sister Mavry. Turns out a feller bumped into them at Walmart and gave 'em the news. They never caught the stranger's name, but they distinctly remember he had a beard, dark sunglasses and wore a shiny hat.

Tea Pain
@TeaPainUSA

Black guy wins by 10 million. GOP calls him "Illegitimate."

White guy loses by 3 million. GOP calls it "Mandate,"
7:15 PM - Dec 18, 2016

💬 454   ↻ 13,900   ♡ 19,456

This says it all, brothers and sisters. Trump won only 304 electoral votes and lost to Hillary by 3 million. Obama won 365 and 332 electoral votes and won by 10 and 5 million respectively. Despite this, Republicans claim Obama wasn't a "legitimate" president, yet Trump's lackluster performance earned him a "mandate."

"No drama Obama" did everything twice as good, yet it still wasn't good enough for a Republican party that is 90% white. Sadly, a black feller's gotta work 3/5ths harder than everybody else just to break even.

Tea Pain
@TeaPainUSA

Trump voters claim they don't hate Obama because he's black. They say they'd hate him just as much if he was Mexican.

11:54 AM - Dec 27, 2016

💬 44   🔁 400   ♡ 1,032

In total fairness, Trump supporters don't only hate minorities. They hate women, too.

Tea Pain
@TeaPainUSA

When someone says they's "sick and tired of bein' politically correct", you know they's just itchin' to call Obama the N-word.

All durin' Obama's presidency, the Tea Party complained about havin' to be "politically correct," but they would never come out and say exactly what that meant. To find out *what it ain't*, we first gotta figure out *what it is*. Political correctness is defined as "the avoidance of language or actions that are seen as excluding, marginalizing or insulting groups of people who are seen as disadvantaged or discriminated against, especially groups defined by sex or race."

Ain't that a kick in the pantaloons? Turns out, *political correctness simply means not bein' a bigoted a-hole.* This sums up the whole Alt-Right movement in a nutshell. Folks who oppose PC want to freely insult, exclude and marginalize folks they consider inferior... which, for them, includes all women and all minorities.

Tea Pain
@TeaPainUSA

In 6 weeks, Trump spent more travel budget than Obama did in a year. His supporters are ok with it since they discovered Trump isn't black.

10:38 AM - Mar 3, 2017

💬 218   🔁 5,225   ♡ 8,217

Golf ain't horse-racin' or falconry, but a lotta folks would argue that golf is a "Sport of Kings"... just not the sport of Rodney King or Martin Luther King. The Tea Party lost their dang minds at the idea of a black president out on a golf course not carryin' some white feller's clubs. But all it took for them to get over it was another white president. (Well, orange.)

As of the writin' of this book, Trump is enjoyin' his 42nd round of golf in just 6 months. Doin' the math, we calculate that Trump will play 672 rounds of golf in 8 years. Obama played only 333 rounds durin' his two terms as president.

Here's a couple of good examples. Take ol' MadBob here. One thing that got ol' Bob madder than a midget with a yo-yo was America's first black president playin' golf!

MadBob @Mad1inUSA · 15 Dec 2015
@Mad1inUSA MORE **FROM** RUSSIA
Obama spent 1,100 hours on **golf** course-equivalent to one-and-a-half months without breaks for sleep or food.

Bob tweeted over 20 times durin' Obama's presidency about his golfin' habits. To Bob, all the world's problems could be solved if Obama sold his clubs on eBay.

Now, since we've established Trump golfs twice as much as Obama did, you know ol' Bob's gotta be beside himself, right? As a matter of fact, since Trump was elected, Bob is so "mad" that he can't even put it into words.

Number of Bob's tweets denouncin' Trump's golfin': zero.

Good news, though! We finally figured out what Bob's really "mad" about.

Sean Hannity ✪ @seanhannity · 19 Aug 2015
.@marklevinshow on @HillaryClinton: "It's time for **Obama** to get off the damn **golf** course & Martha's Vineyard & do something about this."

Sean Hannity ✪ @seanhannity · 30 Sep 2014
Obama was more concerned about his **golf** game than having face-to-face briefings with intel officers on #ISIS. #Hannity

Probably one of the fellers most upset by Obama's abuse of his executive golfin' privileges was ol' Sean Hannity. Sean went on for weeks and months and years about how America was literally burnin' to the ground while Obama lounged on the links.

Sean promised us Trump would fix everything that was wrong with America and, at least for Sean, he was right, cause he's never complained about a President playin' golf or missin' an intel briefin' since. You might even say Sean has a whole new view of America, where right and wrong is as simple as black and white.

Tea Pain
@TeaPainUSA

Trump painted white supremacists as "proud of their heritage." Ownin' humans as property is not a "heritage." It's a "criminal background."

9:32 AM - Aug 13, 2017

💬 120   🔁 2,113   ♡ 4,891

The day of the Charlottesville, Virginia rally, just hours after a Trump-supportin' white supremacist rammed his late-model Dodge Challenger into a crowd of counter-protesters, Trump went on TV and claimed that the white supremacist protesters are "proud of their heritage." To rub salt in the wound, he even said that "hatred and bigoty" came from "many sides." Then, without callin' the enemy by name, he compelled us to accept and love one another.

Trump was "bein' Trump" and did what he did every time his values are challenged: *blame the victims*. Instead of callin' out white supremacists, neo-Nazis and the KKK for the violent racists they are, he blamed the victims instead. In just a few sentences, Trump normalized racism and compelled us to accept and embrace it.

The Alt-Right was ecstatic at Trump's words. The number one neo-Nazi website, "The Daily Stormer," summed it up:

"He said he loved us all. Also refused to answer a question about white supremacists supporting him. No condemnation at all. When asked to condemn, he just walked out of the room. Really, really good. God bless him."

- - -

Alt-Right Now

They're marching out in the streets
With mispelled signs and white sheets
I said "Hey, what is this?"
They're acting like Hitler's SS
I said "Hey what's their name, baby?"
Seems the Tea Party's got a new game
They live on fear, anger and hate
The GOP's the new KKK

They're Alt-Right now, baby they're Alt-Right now
They're Alt-Right now, baby they're Alt-Right now

5. POLITICS

Tea Pain
@TeaPainUSA

It's just plain horse sense. Horse Sense is what a horse has that keeps him from bettin' on people.

This is Tea Pain's favorite sayin'. Tea's granddaddy musta told Tea Pain this a hundred times, and every time Tea Pain would laugh like he never heard it before because he loved his grandpa a lot. Granddaddy Virgil didn't make it past the sixth grade, cause his daddy died from pneumonia when he was 12 and Virgil had to help run the farm. He wasn't educated, but he was smart and he was wise. He taught Tea Pain the value of horse sense.

Lotsa folks mistakenly call horses "dumb animals," but that's far from the truth. Horses are shrewd judges of character; otherwise they wouldn't have survived so long. A horse is a flight animal and has to instantly size up a situation to know whether it's time to run or stay put. Pay close attention to how a feller treats a horse, cause he'll treat a lady the same way. Write that down. It's important.

You can't lie to a horse.

Horses just know stuff. If they get jumpy around one particular feller, there's a reason for it. They read cues that go unnoticed by humans, particularly body language. Humans have a lot of those intuitions, too, except polite society has bred most of it out of us.

To prove Tea's point, think of the last five folks you met. Now think about the impression you got about 'em in the first 90 seconds. Next ask yourself, of those five people, did any of them surprise you and turn out to be the total opposite? Probably not, right?

The good Lord gave us this "horse sense" to protect us from harm. We'd do well to trust this wonderful gift, particularly when it comes to politics.

As a side note, horses don't have mortgage payments, car notes or student loans. They don't get married or divorced. They don't need publicists or attorneys. They don't spend all day on YouTube watchin' crotch-shot fails. Most importantly, you'll never find a horse whose bookie's into him for ten large. So ask yourself, who are the real "dumb animals?"

Tea Pain
@TeaPainUSA

Politics is criticizin' Hillary Clinton for makin' millions while praisin' Donald Trump for makin' billions.

Hypocrisy is nothin' new to politics. As a matter of fact, it's expected. But along came Trump who transformed it into a bona-fide art form. Most savvy politicians choose to ignore hypocrisy by changin' the subject or pointin' to a shinier object, but not Donald Trump. His supporters actually embraced his deliberate hypocrisy and used it as a political tool. They literally waved Trump's blatant hypocrisy in the pundits' faces, then accused the press of bein' "fake news" when they pointed it out.

A perfect example is Hillary's speeches. Ol' HRC made her a nice pile of walkin'-around money from her speech-makin' business. Trump would criticize her ruthlessly on the campaign trail for rakin' in all that dough, then turn around and in the next breath say "I'm really rich," and everyone would cheer. Then he'd tell the folks how they should vote for him because he's way wealthier than the Clintons.

It's like hypocrites had spent the last 200 years in the closet, and they suddenly came out loaded for bear. The reason reasonable folks get upset with hypocrisy is that it insults their intelligence. Trump's tribe proved themselves to be virtually "hypocrisy-proof," cause when it comes to intelligence, they's five beers short of a six pack.

Tea Pain
@TeaPainUSA

Politics is essentially readin' a quote from Adolf Hitler and bein' 100% convinced it's talkin' bout the other party.

Modern politics is no longer about policy and governin' philosophies. It's now the art of comparin' your opponent to Hitler. Tea Pain gets tickled when Democrats and Republicans post the same exact Hitler memes, each 100% convinced in their own minds Hitler was a member of the opposition party.

Hitler and the Nazis are mighty useful tools for the weak-minded. In the same day on Twitter, you'll find conclusive proof the Nazis were "Liberal Democrats" that loved abortion, or "Right Wing fascists" that craved unchecked power. Anti-gay-rights advocates believe whole-heartedly that the Nazis were all homosexuals, while Islamophobes teach that Hitler's inner circle were part of a Muslim "death-cult." That's the beauty of history: there's no one right answer.

Tea Pain
@TeaPainUSA

Politics 101

When GOP controls government, you get fascism.
When DEMs control government, you get health insurance.
3:03 PM - Jul 25, 2017

199   5,940   11,115

Back in the 1980s and 90s, it was pretty hard to tell if we had a Republican president or a Democrat. There weren't near the political contrasts you see today in America. The division really started with Obama, but, to be honest, it wasn't Obama's fault. He couldn't help it if he was a secret Muslim born in Kenya who wasn't legally qualified to be president.

Tea Pain's just pullin' your leg, cause until Obama, no one ever thought twice or questioned whether a president was where he said he was from.

You can imagine just how terrifyin' a young, handsome, well-spoken, charismatic black man was to a lily-white Conservative establishment. He electrified crowds when he spoke. Women fainted. He motivated young folks to vote and be engaged in politics. In essence: the Republicans' worst nightmare. Conservative white racists, who had laid low after sufferin' demoralizin' defeats by the Civil Rights movement, desegregation of schools and Affirmative Action, now saw the sun goin' down on their "silent majority." They felt if they didn't act now and act decisively, they would simply fade to black. Well, uh, anything but black.

Havin' a black president seemed to drive the parties to their respective corners, farther and farther apart on the political spectrum. To make sure nobody confused 'em with the Democrats, the right went about as far right as you could go. So far in fact that they even considered moderate Republicans to be flamin' Liberals.

Obama had a little political capital from his decisive 2008 win, so he decided to spend it on gettin' healthcare for everybody. Even though the idea was essentially taken from Mitt Romney's Massachusetts healthcare plan, the Republicans absolutely hated it for some unspoken reason. As a matter of fact, Mitch McConnell and the Republican leaders got together and agreed that if Obama was for it, they were against it, no matter what it was. And so began the polarization of modern American politics.

Tea Pain
@TeaPainUSA

Q: How many Republicans does it take to screw in a light bulb?
A: We ain't sure, they's too busy screwin' poor folks.

Politics is a lot like street magic. The smooth talkin' magician enchants the crowd with his stagecraft and sleight-of-hand trickery, while his shill moves about the entertained throng, plantin' the card chosen randomly from the stacked deck in an unsuspectin' mark's pocket. The only difference is that, in politics, the shill will steal your wallet while he's at it.

Let's not sugarcoat the process. Millionaires and billionaires are rich because they've figured out a way to get you to give them your money. Even though they have more money than they can ever spend, they delight in findin' new ways to get more.

Take casino magnate Sheldon Adelson, for example. He donated 20 million dollars to Newt Gingrich's long-shot campaign in 2012. Regular folks like us saw that as throwin' money in a hole and settin' it on fire, but that's because we are blinded by the sheer metrics of the matter. If Gingrich pulled off a miracle, his tax policies would have meant over 4 billion - yes, billion with a "b" - in savings for Adelson. Doin' the math, that's a 1 in 200 return for his money. Considerin' ol' Sheldon's massive wealth and holdings, that's the same as us regular folks buyin' a two-dollar lottery ticket.

We're seein' the fruits of those billionaires' investments today in the Trump administration. The first big ticket item on Trump's legislative agenda was the repeal and replacement of Obamacare. This involved realignin' one-sixth of our nation's entire economy. Trump wanted to roll back all the taxes on medical providers and medical instruments. This alone would mean billions of dollars in tax breaks for the richest 1%.

Where do these "tax savings" come from? Well, they gotta come from somewhere, and you can guess where: *from poor folks*. Over 20 million poor and middle class folks would lose their healthcare, but look on the bright side: somewhere a CEO is gettin' a sweet new yacht.

Tea Pain
@TeaPainUSA

How many Conservatives does it take to change a light bulb?
None. They hate change.#GOPDebate #TeaTweets

We overlooked a part of the process: how the richest folks use politicians to get your money. It's pretty simple. You have to vote for the horses they're backin'. So how does this work? How do they get folks to vote *against their own best interests*?

It's simpler than you think and employs the use of the world's oldest emotion: *fear*. Simply put, politics plays to our most primal, basest fears.

In the early days of man, before the great civilizations emerged, we were a bunch of smaller tribes. We swore our loyalty to our village and knew our best chance to survive was standin' by our little group against whatever threatened our gates. This is known as tribalism, and it's as alive and well today as it's ever been… except today we pledge support to political tribes instead.

A politician can't just come out and say, "Hey, give me your vote so my rich overlords can take more of your money." Instead they distract you by targetin' your most basic fears. Even though they use more flowery language, they are essentially sayin', "Vote for me, or the feller from that other village will come and take away our weapons, and we'll all die!" Or they appeal to our tribal patriotism through fear. "We need to take America back from that other tribe, cause if we don't, God's gonna kill us all."

More recently, they challenge our deepest sexual fears. "If you don't vote for me, a tribe of gay folks are gonna come and make you gay-marry a feller named Steve!"

That's it, friends. Rich folks have been playin' the "God, Guns and Gays" card against the weak-minded since Tea Pain was poopin' his Pampers. They like what they've got goin'. It's a sweet deal, and they'll spend lotsa money they just took from you to keep it that way!

Tea Pain
@TeaPainUSA

Politics is all about timin'. If Ted Cruz were president 30 years ago, he wouldn't have let his Dad into the country. #CruzCrew @TedCruz

Until Donald Trump came along, Ted Cruz was the de facto racist leader of the far right. What better feller was there to lead the charge against the brown-skinned menace than a Canadian-born Cuban?

Ted paints in hypocrisy like Monet painted in watercolors. Accordin' to Ted, Obama was a foreign-born son of a Communist revolutionary, unlike Ted, who was a foreign-born son of a

Communist revolutionary. Ted constantly preached the "fall of America" was due to Obama's out-of-control immigration policies, and we must close down all the borders immediately or there'd be "taco trucks on every corner." Tea Pain loves tacos and never understood the downside of ready access to delicious Mexican cuisine.

Tea Partiers loved ol' Ted for his crazy ideas and his carefully coded racist dog whistles. Funny thing, if Richard Nixon held Ted's views on immigration, his family would have never been allowed to move here in the first place and Ted would never have become a Texas Senator. Fortunately, Ted never asked his supporters to think, just vote.

Tea Pain
@TeaPainUSA

BREAKING: Ted Cruz to support Trump. Trump now claims Cruz's dad didn't shoot JFK, merely bought Oswald the rifle.
1:31 PM - Sep 23, 2016

💬 57   🔁 444   ♡ 836

You almost gotta feel bad for Teddy Cruz. He had such big dreams. His daddy and all the wackadoodles in the Christian Dominion movement assured Ted that God had anointed him to be the next president of the United States and deliver us from the Antichrist Barack Obama.

Ted knew what his Christian base truly craved: a white messiah that would lead America back to the white Christian nation that Jesus died on the cross for. Ted honed his racially coded homilies, shut down the government once and was leadin' the charge against gay marriage. Everything was goin' Ted's way - that is, until Donald Trump showed up.

It was leaked recently that Ted Cruz appeared on an episode of Celebrity Apprentice once, but that scene ended up on the cuttin' room floor and never made it to TV. It went something like this:

TRUMP: *Tell me, Ted. How is your project coming along?*

CRUZ: *Very well, Donald. I've spent three years carefully codifying a racial code that allows me to appeal to the bigoted fears of the far-right and their natural resentment of minorities.*

TRUMP: *Boo-hoo! I did that in one afternoon in Phoenix. You're fired!*

Tea Pain
@TeaPainUSA

Sorry folks, but Meals on Wheels ain't workin'. They feed seniors one day and by the next day they're hungry again. #Budget2017

4:37 PM - Mar 16, 2017

565   8,712   17,057

Growin' up, we always had plenty to eat and had clothes to wear and we felt mighty blessed for it, but still we were never all that far from the poor house. Once, Tea's daddy got laid off at the sawmill for a couple months, and there was some tough sleddin' for a while. If it weren't for his unemployment insurance and a little help from the food-stamp folks, no tellin' what would have happened to the Pain clan.

Conservatives look down their noses at these programs, callin' them "entitlements." Tea Pain's gonna lay it out straight for ya. Daddy worked for 47 years payin' into these "entitlement" programs, only to take a fraction back in return. If anybody was ever "entitled" to use 'em, it was him!

Brother Jesus was clear about how He felt about poor folks: "Blessed are the poor, for yours is the kingdom of God." - Luke 6:20. It's sad how Conservative "Christians," who stand on street corners and make long prayers, are the first ones to take away help for poor folks while givin' tax cuts to millionaires and billionaires.

Tea Pain
@TeaPainUSA

Watergate, 9/11, Katrina & #TrumpRussia. When you think about it, without GOP Presidents we'd have no scandals to compare the next one to.
12:58 PM - Jun 21, 2017

💬 118   🔁 1,082   ♡ 2,464

Remember when Conservatives were desperately searchin' for any scandal they could link to no-drama Obama? Try as they may, they could never fabricate "Obama's Katrina" or "Obama's 9/11." That got ol' Tea Pain to thinkin': all the epic scandals in modern politics are owned by Republicans. Thanks to Nixon, all you gotta do is stick "gate" on the end of anything, and you got yourself a scandal! One day, Conservatives will bash Michelle Obama's second term askin' if this is "Michelle Obama's #TrumpRussia" or have we just witnessed "Michelle Obama's Access Hollywood Moment?"

Tea Pain
@TeaPainUSA

Politics today is mostly fightin' over which crooked politician we like the best. #TeaBomb

Tea Pain is more of a left-center kinda feller by nature, mainly because he wants equality for everybody and he thinks it's the best direction for our great nation - but he ain't so blind to think that his party does no wrong. This is politics after all. Even the best politician has trouble with the truth now and then.

Back in the late 1890s, cotton was king in the South. It was the most valuable and lucrative of all the cash crops and propped up a large portion of the Southern economy. That is, until the arrival of the brown Mexican boll weevil. Them little insect-critters hitchhiked up this way from Mexico, hop-scotchin' from one farm truck to another, then from one field to the next, till they slowly infested virtually every cotton field in the South. They were immune to insecticides and decimated the cotton harvest for years.

One feller found a way to cash in on this disaster. Ben Rothman was a local ne'er-do-well whose biggest success in life was managin' to marry the local spinster, Terri Brannen. "Little Bennie," as he was known, was always workin' on one get-rich-quick scheme after another, quickly burnin' through his wife's savings, till one day he stumbled onto a vision that made him rich.

Little Bennie got the idea to build a boll weevil racetrack. He converted an old suitcase into a "Rothman Downs." He caught some of the biggest of the boll weevils and painted little numbers on 'em. Inside the suitcase he fashioned a little track with a rail and everything. There was a little gate he could open, and off they'd go! Cotton farmers would come from miles around to lay down the rest of their rent money, hopin' to improve their saggin' fortunes on Bennie's little enterprise.

"Tough times always brings out the chumps," Little Bennie used to say. Bennie kept the fastest weevils for himself and got a cut of all the action, so he raked it in hand over fist.

"Weevil Knievel" - Undefeated Weevil Racing Champion
1902 - B. Rothman, owner.

As the project grew, Bennie tried to heighten the realism of the experience by trainin' mosquitos to ride on the backs of the boll weevils like little jockeys, but he soon gave up on this because he couldn't make a ridin' crop small enough for the skeeters to carry, so they looked silly just sittin' there.

Long story short, Bennie became richer than George Foreman on his invention - that is, until the Feds discovered he was nine years delinquent on back taxes and locked him up in the Cummins Detention Unit down in Grady. Back in the '20s, Tea Pain's Grandpa Virgil went there to visit one of his rowdy cousins doin' a five year stretch for breakin' and enterin'. Just so happened his cellmate was one "Little Bennie" Rothman. Bennie regaled Grandpa Virgil with the whole saga of Rothman Downs and his weevil-racin' empire.

Virgil, always polite, indulged Bennie a little and asked him what was the secret to his "success." Bennie looked Virgil straight in the eye and said, "Virgil, it's just like politics. You gotta learn to pick the lesser of two weevils."

- - -

Tea Pain
@TeaPainUSA

#FridayRep Tea Pain's "trumpin'" the Donald in this smokin' remix, "Dancin' in the Street." @RealDonaldTrump

Dancin' in the Street
Tea & the Paindellas

Callin' out around the land
Are you ready for a new Trump treat?
On nine-eleven he saw thousands
Dancing in the street

They're dancin' in New Jersey
Down in Newark, too
East of New York City

All he sees is Muslims, yeah Muslims
There's Muslims everywhere
Towers fallin', Allah Akbar-in'
And dancin' in the street

Oh, it doesn't matter if it's true
As long as the fear gets through
So come on, every nut grab a gun
The end times have begun!

They're dancin' in the street.

6. GOD

Tea Pain
@TeaPainUSA

BIBLE BASICS FOR BEGINNERS: New Testament is
Disney. Old Testament is Tarantino. #ccot

They say there's two things you should never talk about: politics
and religion. Take them two away, and Twitter would be a vast
wasteland bereft of interest and entertainment. It would be nothin'
but a montage of Kardashian selfies and adorable little kitty cat
videos. Tea Pain believes there ain't nothin' too scary to talk about,
so here goes!

Tea Pain's fondest memories of church was sittin' in the pew on
Sunday mornin' next to Mama and Daddy, listenin' to the stories
about Brother Jesus healin' folks and tellin' parables about sheep
and goats and other critters. It made Tea Pain feel mighty special to
know that the Great Creator that breathed all things into existence
could still care about a little poot like him. One of Tea's favorite
hymns was "His Eye Is On the Sparrow." It was a sho nuff
comfortin' feelin' when we all sang *"His eye is on the sparrow, and I
know He watches me."* From early on, Tea Pain came to believe
religion should comfort folks, not scare 'em to death.

Tea Pain
@TeaPainUSA

Conservatives say the problem is Christianity ain't taught in schools. The real problem is Christianity ain't taught in church.

8:27 AM - Apr 18, 2015   ♡ 848   ⟲ 9,044   ♡ 11,596

If it don't happen to be Sunday mornin' when you're readin' this, forgive ol' Tea Pain, cause he's naturally gotta preach.

First, let's be clear. Schools are for teachin' the three Rs: Readin', Ritin' and Rithmetic. If you're blamin' the American public school system for not teachin' kids about your religion, then you've already admitted you've failed as a church and as a parent.

If it's the school's job to teach religion, then you shouldn't mind if they teach Islam, Judaism or Buddhism too, right? What's that you say? School's should only teach the "Christian" religion? Then which of the 31,000 Christian denominations should the school teach? Southern Baptist? Lutheran? Catholic? Jehovah's Witness?

There's a good reason most Christians are Bible illiterates these days. Many of the big churches they go to are worried more about entertainment and politics than religion. For example, there's this mega-church up in Springfield that has bowlin' alleys, a movie theatre, even a computer lab, but they had to cancel Wednesday night Bible study due to lack of attendance.

But when there was a referendum to remove a city-ordinance that protected gay folks from bein' fired simply for bein' gay, this same Goliath Baptist Church organized a bussin' program that General Patton would have been envious of. As a result, these good "Christians" stole basic civil rights from innocent gay folks, just like Jesus taught 'em to do.

Apparently churches are too busy "doin' the Lord's work" to teach the Bible, so they say the school system needs to pick up the slack.

Fortunately, our forefathers wisely created a system that guarantees religious freedom for everyone, not just the majority religion at the moment. That's the beauty of America. Its public school system attempts to abide by the United States Constitution. It's a novel concept more folks should try sometime! Sorry churches, as much a burden as it may be, it's gonna be up to you to teach the Bible for a while longer.

Tea Pain
@TeaPainUSA

If you're usin' Christianity to get even, you ain't usin' it right. #tcot #prolife #ccot #Bible

10:07 AM - Jun 11, 2015

One of the biggest burrs under Tea Pain's saddle are loudmouth Christian Conservatives beatin' their chests and a'thumpin' their Bibles, especially when these folks ain't cracked the Good Book in 20 years. As Tea Pain likes to say, they "don't know their Bible from a backhoe!"

Now don't get Tea Pain wrong. There's millions of good Christians quietly livin' lives of faith and doin' untold good in this world. But nothin' gets Tea Pain's hackles up like some ol' Philistine dishonorin' the Good Lord with the hateful misuse of His word.

It was for this reason that Tea Pain created *"The Bible Knowledge Cage Match."*

Tea Pain @TeaPainUSA · 28 Sep 2016
Tea Pain's Bible Cage claims another phony Trump "Christian". -> @realdcm <-
He fled like a **scalded cat** after just one **question**!

Tea Pain challenges you to a

Bible Knowledge Cage Match

Conor
@realdcm

You are blocked from following @realdcm

Tea Pain got real tired real fast of Christian phonies beatin' up on Tea Pain's Twitter pals about politics while contortin' scripture to back their Tea Party nutballery. One day, Tea Pain had enough of this foolishness and started callin' out these Judas goats to step into the Bible Cage with Tea Pain. Funny thing, these self-righteous bullies are no different than any other playground thug. The first time someone stands up to 'em, they run like a scalded Hittite.

Tea Pain don't like to brag, but he's read the Good Book from Genesis to Revelations more times than he can remember. Tea Pain lives by 2 Timothy 2:15: "Study to show thyself approved unto God, a workman that needeth not to be ashamed, rightly dividing the word of truth." As a result, it don't take long for Tea Pain to separate the wheat from the chaff in a Bible tussle.

All in all, Tea Pain has issued over 300 "Cage Matches," and as you'd expect, almost every one of them ol' scudders ran like a jack rabbit! The few foolish enough to step in soon found themselves in a world of Pain.

If you're gonna go on Twitter and start braggin' about what a good Christian you are and what sinners other folks are, then you've been readin' your Bible upside down. The worst is the Christian CEOs: "Christmas and Easter Only." If you darken the church doorways twice a year, then consider Christianity your "hobby," not your faith. Follerin' Jesus ain't like the hokey-pokey. You don't put your big toe in, then put your big toe out; you jump in with both feet.

Until then, check your self-righteousness at the door, cause when Tea Pain finds you, he's gonna lay an epic #BibleThumpin' on ya!

Tea Pain
@TeaPainUSA

Conservatives say "Islam wants you dead for not believin' in Islam", while Christianity only requires unbelievers to writhe in eternal hell.

9:16 AM - Aug 10, 2017

💬 112   🔁 548   ♡ 1,878

When you study the Old Testament, you quickly find out the good Lord has a lotta different names, such as "Jehovah," "Eloah," "Elohim" and "El Shaddai." You probably remember from Sunday School that Father Abraham had two sons, Isaac and Ishmael. Isaac was the patriarch of the Hebrews, and Ishmael was the father of the Arabs. Since Judaism and Islam both had the same daddy, it's silly to think there'd be a vast difference between the two.

Tea Pain's figured out the real bone of contention between Conservative Christianity and Islam: they're too similar and they's just fightin' over market share.

One thing that tickles Tea Pain is that Twitter Christians claim "Allah" is a "false god," and that Islam is a Satanic cult. Wanna know the real joke? It turns out the Arabic "Allah" and the Hebrew "Eloah" come from the same Chaldean word "El," simply meanin' "God." Allah and Elohim are the same deity. Heck, they even came from the same hometown. Ain't that a kick in the pants? If Conservatives ever stopped to think, they'd be mighty uncomfortable to find out they walk hand-in-hand with Muhammad on guns, abortion, gays, submissive women and religious laws.

How many times have you heard Twitter Christians call Muslims "savages," because the Koran says unbelievers should be put to death? Christianity has a much kinder, more benevolent vision where unbelievers writhe in an eternal torment of unquenchable hell-fire, their souls roastin' in the same holy spittle as Hitler, Bonnie and Clyde and the feller that wrote the season finale of Dexter.

U.S. ABORTIONS BY RELIGION *

Protestant 37.4%

Catholic: 31.3%

None: 23.7%

Evangelical: 18%

Jewish: 1.3%

@TeaPainUSA — Source: Antiochian Orthodox Christian Archdiocese

* A number of women identified as both Protestant and Evangelical

Tea Pain got mighty tired of Conservatives callin' Liberals "baby killers" whenever they were on the losin' end of an argument, which - come to think of it - was most of the time. They seem to actually believe just because you think a woman should have control over her body that you're a "godless atheist that delights in the murder of babies."

Tea Pain ain't a fan of guilt. Misused, it's one of the deadliest weapons out there, so Tea decided to get the facts on who uses abortion. The numbers'll blow your hair straight back. The gist of the women folks that have abortions are primarily Christians! When you consider that 83% of Americans identify as Christian, it makes perfect sense. Turns out, "godless atheists" make up less than a fourth. Like Tea Pain says in the 7 Tenets of Americanism: "A woman's body is hers… period!"

Tea Pain
@TeaPainUSA

If abortion is murder then women would be subject to the death penalty. Ain't #ProLife politics confusin'?

Now here's one of the biggest riddles on Twitter. Pro-lifers call abortion "murder." The penalty for premeditated murder is death; therefore, those who cherish the sanctity of life are callin' for women to be put to death… which ain't pro-life, is it? Next time you get called a "baby killer," have fun with this little Twitter-twister.

Tea Pain @TeaPainUSA · 27 Jan 2016
CHECK IT OUT: Tea Pain just met the nicest Conservative "Christian" who believes in **abortion**. -> @mance1950

j r nance @mance1950 · 34m
@TeaPainUSA We Hate All POS Libs like you, your mother should have aborted you & the world would have been a better place, 1 less Lib!!

Every now and then you run into a Twitter Christian that believes in abortion, but only for those they don't like. These folks will tell you in one breath that all men are created equal. By this they mean "equal lookin'," "equal actin'" and "equal thinkin'" to folks like them. Everybody else is on their own. Folks like this put the "Duh" in "Democracy."

Christine Marat
@kyramarat1

Orthodox Christian Far Right. BFA. MFA.
Pro-gun and vets. I hate liberalism. Am
totally politically incorrect. TRUMP.
Followed by Roger J Stone

Christine Marat @kyramarat1 · 30m
It took awhile but we're fighting back. We're white, we're right and we'll
fight #WhiteGenocide

Christine Marat @kyramarat1 · Oct 15
DS EXCLUSIVE: The Jews Behind the Latest Trump Defamation and the Crazy
Leftist Who Lied for Them – **Daily Stormer**

Christine Marat @kyramarat1 · Dec 22
Thank you for speaking for your community and clarifying **Jews** hate white
people.

Christine Marat @kyramarat1 · 3m
@badzenmonk @zlando @GenoGuzman1 so stupid. And the jews lap
it up

Ever wonder why almost every neo-Nazi or Alt-Right white
supremacist you see on Twitter is a Christian? Tea Pain wonders
the same thing.

Take ol' Christine here. Not only is she Twitter-pals with Trump
aide Roger Stone, but when she's not readin' her Bible, she's on
white supremacist websites learnin' about Jewish folks.

How these folks can be both a racist and a "Christian" at the same
time is a mystery. First, they worship heavenly Jesus as a deity, but
they'd stick the earthly Jesus on the "Do Not Fly" list in a
heartbeat and ban him from ever settin' foot in America if they
could. They just can't trust dark-skinned foreigners that embrace
radical Middle Eastern religions.

Second of all, the Bible calls Jesus "King of the Jews," even though
accordin' to them, the Jews "corrupt our youth by runnin'
Hollywood, the press and the bankin' systems." You see, when you
mix politics and religion together, things can get mighty confusin'.
But, when you stop and think about it for just a second, one
mystery does become a little bit clearer. We can now see why neo-

Nazis would really enjoy the Christmas story of a brown-skinned Jewish refugee family bein' turned away from the inn and havin' to sleep in the barn with the rest of the animals.

Tea Pain
@TeaPainUSA

Donald Trump is obviously a Christian and a big fan of the Bible. His favorite passage is Chapter 11.

Granted, this is more of a Trump joke than a Bible Thumper joke, but Tea Pain really wanted to include it. Tea Pain's book, Tea Pain's rules.

Tea Pain
@TeaPainUSA

Mississippi Gov. Phil Bryant signs religious freedom bill into law. Now Christians are free to ignore the law & the Bible at the same time.

12:46 PM - Apr 5, 2016

♡ 12   ♺ 328   ♡ 342

Have you noticed that everything in politics is mislabeled?

Right-to-Work, Fair-Tax and Affordable Care Act spring to mind, and now: Religious Freedom Act. We need to call this law by its true name: the "Lettin' Bigots Oppress Folks Different Than Them Act." The Bible teaches us to all be messengers of the Word and bring the Good News to others through the way we live our lives and our kind works. This, of course, is a lotta work for Twitter Christians; so instead, they vote for folks that pass laws that let 'em be mean to the very folks they should be ministerin' to.

Folks that study history know that first century Christians suffered great persecutions at the hands of evil men. Some were crucified, others set on fire, some even fed to the lions before the blood-thirsty crowds in the Colosseum. But none of these early saints were faced with the terrifyin' temptation of havin' to bake a cake for a lesbian couple or make pizzas for a gay weddin' reception.

Thanks to modern-day Conservatism, Twitter Christians are now protected by laws that reflect Jefferson's immortal words, "We hold these truths to be self-evident, that all men are created equal, that they are endowed by their Creator with certain unalienable Rights, that among these are Life, Liberty and the *freedom not to treat folks we don't like as humans.*"

 Tea Pain @TeaPainUSA · 28 Sep 2016
You really think the **Bible** is "pro-life"?

Is the Bible "Pro-Life?"

Give them, Lord—
what will you give them?
Give them wombs that miscarry
and breasts that are dry.
Hosea 9:14

The people of Samaria must bear their
guilt, because they have rebelled
against their God. They will fall by the
sword; their little ones will be dashed
to the ground, their pregnant women
ripped open.
Hosea 13:16

God's instructions to Moses about the Midianites

Now kill all the boys. And kill every
woman who has slept with a man,
but save for yourselves every girl
who has never slept with a man.
Numbers 31:17-18

Now go and attack Amalek, and utterly
destroy all that they have, and do not
spare them. But kill both man and
woman, infant and nursing child, ox
and sheep, camel and donkey.
1st Samuel 15:3

Daughter Babylon, doomed to destruction, happy is the one who repays you
according to what you have done to us. Happy is the one who seizes your infants
and dashes them against the rocks.
Psalms 137:8-9

Ever talk to a pro-lifer for very long? When you ask them for the authority to back up their arguments, they turn to the worst text possible for help: the Bible.

There's a literal river of blood that runs through the Old Testament. When you do the math, you find there are 158 God-sanctioned murders that affected almost 25 million folks. Many of these folks were women and children. Even pregnant women weren't spared from the genocide God ordered the "chosen people" to commit on their neighbors, simply because they believed in a different God. Today, that would be like justifyin' murder simply because somebody doesn't like Game of Thrones.

When you talk to a pro-lifer, ask 'em the follerin' questions:

1. Do you support Capital Punishment?
2. Do you support war against our enemies?
3. Do you believe in protectin' your homes and property with deadly force?

Turns out pro-lifers ain't pro-life at all. They's "pro-birth." They don't give two shucks about the baby once it's born; they just wanna make sure the woman pays for her "sin" of sexual pleasure. See if Tea Pain ain't tellin' you the truth! Pregnancy and labor is "punishment" for her sins. Abortion is lettin' her escape her "sentence."

Tea Pain's mama was an extra-special lady. She taught him to love and respect all women, though in fairness to Mama, she never heard of Ann Coulter. A woman has to bear the double-portion of the burdens in this life, especially dealin' with deadbeat dads and boyfriends that disappear if she turns up pregnant. Makin' sure women have the final say about their reproductive decisions is the *very least* a free society can do.

Tea Pain
@TeaPainUSA

Now that #KimDavis is an elected official that won't do her job, she's been made an honorary member of Congress.
11:33 AM - Sep 14, 2015

💬 25   🔁 330   ♡ 438

In Kim Davis's wildest dreams, she never imagined she'd become a martyr for all the "persecuted Christians" in America. Kim became famous overnight for her refusal to foller the newly minted Supreme Court rulin' that allowed gay folks to get married. Not "Honey Boo Boo" famous, but purty close.

Kim was a court clerk in Rowan County, Kentucky. Claimin' she was "acting under God's authority," she reacted by denyin' marriage licenses to EVERYBODY. This won her a free, all-expense paid trip to the Rowan County pokey. The media then descended en-masse on the little courthouse. The circus had come to town, and with it came the clowns. Smellin' an opportunity to make a little political hay, Mike Huckabee and Ted Cruz vied daily to become Ms. Davis's newest best friends. They took turns transformin' themselves into modern day John the Baptists, cryin' and catterwallin' in the wilderness, lamentin' the destitute soul of the godless United States government.

It only took a little diggin' to hit a political septic tank. Turns out, Saint Kim had enjoyed three failed marriages, and she was on her fourth with one of the aforementioned three husbands. If only Kim had encountered someone like herself when she was younger, someone "actin' under God's authority" to deny her those marriage licenses because they believed the Bible forbid divorce, it might have saved her thousands in legal fees and some mighty awkward Father's Day celebrations.

- - -

Ooh, Kim is bigger
Bigger than the law
And the Supreme Court
Those gays they can't get hitched
It's evil in God's eyes
But she said too much, they locked her up.

That's Kim on the TV
That's Kim in the spotlight
Usin' her religion
They elected her to do her job
But she says she won't do it
Oh no she said too much
She hasn't said enough
We heard she signed a book deal
We know that she make millions
We know you'll get a gig on Fox

T.E.A.

USIN' 'MY' RELIGION

Tea Pain
@TeaPainUSA

#FridayRap This week, Tea Pain's rappin' on #KimDavis in the bangin' R.E.M. remix.

8:49 AM - Sep 18, 2015

💬 5   🔁 25   ♡ 27

7. GUNS

We'll find a way for you to keep your guns if you find a way for us to keep our kids.

Nothin' breaks Tea Pain's heart more than news of a school shootin'. Them poor kids, full of hope and promise, their whole lives ahead of them, struck down before they even got started. It's a cryin' shame.

Conscientious folks that fight to prevent the next shootin' must ultimately do battle with the NRA, one of the most well-organized, best-financed political lobbies in America.

Before we jump into one of the most hotly contested political issues on social media, Tea Pain's gonna take us to church on the second amendment.

> *"A well-regulated Militia, being necessary to the security of a free State, the right of the people to keep and bear Arms, shall not be infringed."*
> 2nd Amendment, U.S. Constitution

Tea Pain would wager you that 98% of "Second Amendment enthusiasts" have never read the entire Constitution. To top that, Tea'd bet you even money less than half of those folks ain't never read the entire Second Amendment for that matter, cause it's easily one of the most tortured sentences in the history of the English language.

Now Tea Pain ain't no scholar, but he worked awfully hard to get his GED. Not to brag, but he was the first Pain to ever have one. Gettin' it before his 41st birthday was just icin' on the cake!

One of the things Tea Pain remembered from his book learnin' was sentence structure. There's subjects, verbs, objects, nouns... all kinds of interestin' stuff. One of the things they teach you is that the subject of a sentence is usually near the beginnin'. The Second Amendment is a perfect example: "A well-regulated Militia".

Now if the Second Amendment was supposed to give folks the right to tote their guns to Chipotle, don't you reckon it would have said that instead? See, it's mighty clear we're talkin' about local and state militias. And not just any militia, mind you, but a "well-regulated" one. "Well-regulated" refers to rules and policies, controls over how the militia is to act and behave. Ain't it funny that the one part of the Constitution that allegedly gives everyone unregulated gun rights has the phrase "well-regulated" in it?

Now ask yourself another question. If gun rights were the cornerstone of Constitutional freedom, why did they "forget" to put it in the first draft? They actually had to include it later as an amendment, an afterthought. There's a simple reason for that: *The Second Amendment has nothin' to do with private gun ownership!*

If these hillbilly "Constitutional experts" had actually studied American history, they'd know that ol' King George had outlawed state militias, due to the fact they were part of the colonial rebellion against the crown. The framers of the Constitution became concerned that one day an American "king" might rise wishin' to do the same thing to protect his own abuse of power. So they made sure that well-regulated militias were codified in writin' - that way Americans were guaranteed by law that they could protect themselves against tyranny. And that, friends, is why the Second Amendment was born: to allow us to bear arms to protect our "free state," but within the bounds of a well-regulated militia. See how simple things can be when you just read the words and know a little history?

Then what about gun rights? Are we allowed to own guns to hunt and protect ourselves with? You're dang right we are, because guns are covered under normal private property laws just like everything else we own. The government has no more right to take away our guns than our television sets or our blenders.

When Tommy Jefferson helped draft the Virginia Constitution, he wrote, "*No freeman shall be debarred the use of arms within his own lands or tenements.*" Just like Tea Pain said. Guns is for huntin' and protectin' and are covered under laws of personal property. But outside of our "lands or tenements," gun use is within the purview of federal, state and local governments.

People will fuss at Tea Pain and say this "weakens" gun rights. Oh contraire, mon pare! There is no stronger cornerstone to the United States Constitution than ownership of personal property! America's founders understood clearly that private property is the foundation not only of prosperity but of freedom itself. True gun enthusiasts would be wise to line up behind this immovable pillar of American democracy and stop torturin' the poor Second Amendment!

When Wyatt, Virgil and Morgan Earp tried to keep the peace durin' the Wild, Wild West out in Tombstone, Arizona, they made a law that it was illegal to carry guns outside of your home within the confines of Tombstone city limits. No one would ever accuse Wyatt Earp of bein' a gun hatin' liberal, at least not to his face. That law was within their jurisdiction and never violated the personal property laws of gun ownership. In closin', Tea Pain's gonna use one of the Republican's most beloved arguments against 'em. Gun use, outside of our homes and property, is most often a matter of "states' rights."

That's not to say that states have sole jurisdiction over gun regulations, but - referencin' the 10th Amendment - anything not covered by the federal government is automatically left up to the states to decide. To sum up, private gun ownership is rock solid. Takin' your guns to town, on the other hand, is up to federal, state and local governments. Yes, patriots, it's that simple.

Tea Pain
@TeaPainUSA

Trump claims Obama will never say "Radical Islamic Terrorism", but notice how Trump never says "Religious Fanatic Gun Lovers?"

11:06 PM - Jun 12, 2016

💬 32   🔁 490   ♡ 677

Trump blew his racist dog whistle every chance he got during the 2016 presidential campaign. To hear Trump tell it, Muslims were hidin' behind every door, ready to slit our throats. He claimed that mosques were fulla hate and needed to be shuttered, yet he let one domestic shootin' after another go without comment. Considerin' there are over 30,000 gun deaths a year in America, "radical gun nuts," not "radical Islamic terrorism," are America's biggest enemy.

Tea Pain
@TeaPainUSA

More Muslims have been killed by Trump supporters in the past 24 hours than Americans killed by refugees from banned countries in 30 years.

1:02 PM - Jan 30, 2017

543 42,881 59,575

On January 29, 2017, shortly after Trump's inauguration, Alexandre Bissonnette walked into an Islamic Cultural Centre in Quebec City wearing a black ski mask, shoutin' "Allah Akbar" and cuttin' loose with his CZ 858 assault rifle and 9 millimeter semi-automatic pistol. When the smoke cleared, six lay dead and 19 were injured.

Turns out Bissonnette was a "kid" in his mid-twenties with no criminal record. The news reported he was a recent wide-eyed convert to white nationalism thanks to Donald Trump and French far-right nutball Marine LePen. The hate wasn't comin' from the mosques, as Trump said, but was bein' poured out in full measure on the mosques by Trump's corrupted disciples.

Trump continued to call for a "Muslim Ban," justifyin' it with stories about how refugees from certain Muslim-majority countries posed a "grave threat to national security." Sadly, Trumpanistas overlooked one sad truth. In one day, Trump supporters had killed more Muslims than all Americans killed by refugees from the "Muslim Ban" countries in 30 years.

Tea Pain
@TeaPainUSA

New law says "If you're crazy enough vote for Trump, you're crazy enough to own a gun."

10:49 AM - Feb 3, 2017

💬 32   🔁 343   ♡ 429

One of the first things Trump undid as president was the law prohibitin' mentally disabled people from ownin' guns. Apparently, crazy folks have just as much right to shoot up the mall as anyone else, plus that "mentally disabled" part was hittin' a little too close to home for Trump's base.

After the spate of shootings by mentally-ill sickos like Robert Lewis Dear and Dylann Roof, you would think Conservatives would want to do the right thing and keep guns outta the hands of wackos. True enough, it might be the right thing to do, but it ain't the far-right thing to do!

Tea Pain
@TeaPainUSA

New Trump 2nd Amendment stance. "The only way to stop a bad man with a gun is a white man with a gun."

Even though Ammosexuals are vehemently opposed to gun control, they do admit there might a time and a place for it. In certain cases, takin' away guns may actually be a good thing, provided you take 'em away from the right people.

Tea Pain @TeaPainUSA · 23 Sep 2016
Donald **Trump** has finally found a way to silence the gun nuts. Tell 'em you're takin' away **guns** from black folks. #NRA #Gunsense

"If they see a person possibly with a gun or they think may have a gun, they will see the person and they'll look and *they'll take the gun away.*"

Trump reached deep into the Republican Jim Crow goodie bag and pulled out a dusty ol' jewel: *stop and frisk*. This practice was abandoned years ago, because it was deemed as unconstitutional and never had any tangible results on public safety... which made it a perfect slogan for Trump's white nationalist campaign. It might as well have been labeled for what it really was: racial profilin'. Ol Chris Matthews always tickled Tea Pain when he'd say, "These aren't racist dog whistles; they're racist car alarms!"

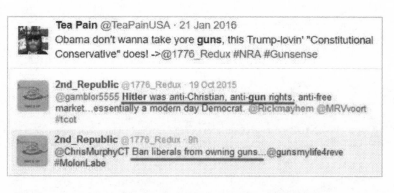

Tea Pain @TeaPainUSA · 21 Jan 2016
Obama don't wanna take yore **guns**, this Trump-lovin' "Constitutional Conservative" does! ->@1776_Redux #NRA #Gunsense

2nd_Republic @1776_Redux · 19 Oct 2015
@gamblor5555 **Hitler was anti-Christian, anti-gun rights**, anti-free market...essentially a modern day Democrat. @Rickmayhem @MRVvoort #tcot

2nd_Republic @1776_Redux · 9h
@ChrisMurphyCT Ban liberals from owning guns... @gunsmylife4reve #MolonLabe

Every now and then, Tea Pain would encounter a gun nut to end all gun nuts. Such is 2nd Republic. If you didn't like what he said in one tweet, stick around, cause he'd usually contradict it with the next. Let's dissect these two beauties, because what they lack in consistency, they more than make up for with historical inaccuracies.

First, Hitler was Catholic and even went so far as to proclaim Christianity as the national religion of Germany. The 24th tenet of the Nazi "Constitution" stated, "The Party as such advocates the standpoint of a positive Christianity without binding itself confessionally to any one denomination."

Hitler was not "anti-gun rights" at all, provided you were Aryan; those folks enjoyed relaxed gun restrictions. But Hitler took away guns from "unreliable persons" such as Jews, gypsies, etc. Now here's where 2nd Republic goes off the rails. In one breath he calls Hitler a "modern-day Democrat" for takin' away folks' guns, then turns around in the next tweet and demands that guns be taken away from Democrats! Ol' Joe Goebbels would be so proud!

(Fun side note: 2nd Republic was banned previously from Twitter for death threats, then his current account was locked due to promotion of Nazi propaganda from a number of white supremacist websites.)

Tea Pain
@TeaPainUSA

Thanks to the #NRA, just because you can't fly on the plane don't mean you can't buy a gun a shoot up the airport. #Gunsense

If there was ever a "Sophie's Choice" for Conservatives, this is it. There was some pendin' legislation in Congress sayin' you couldn't buy a gun if you were on the "Do Not Fly" list. On one hand, Alt-Righties would love nothin' more than to strip away rights from Muslims, but, on the other hand, what if that dictator Obama decided to put the whole Tea Party on the DNF list? Then he could take away all their guns just like he'd been promisin' for years! Dang! That was a close one. That sneaky Obama almost pulled the wool over their eyes on that one!

All Tea Pain can say is this: bigots must really love their guns when they pass up the chance to take stuff away from Mohammed's kinfolks.

 Tea Pain
@TeaPainUSA

Q: What's the difference between voters and gun owners?
A: Republicans don't suppress gun ownership.
11:10 PM - Jun 30, 2017

♡ 76   ↻ 1,769   ♡ 3,869

There are over 30,000 gun deaths in the U.S. annually, but less than 10 incidents of voter fraud. Republicans point out that this fraud tends to occur mostly in "inner cities," so you can probably guess what the real tragedy in America is. Yep, that's right: minorities votin'.

 Tea Pain
@TeaPainUSA

Tea Party Gun Nuts say school shootins result from no prayer in schools. Then explain a church shootin'! #NRA #TCOT #Gunsense

---

There's a sad ol' political tactic that works on the weak-minded: blamin' the victims. You know all those innocent kids that have been lost in school shootings? We'll it's their fault for not prayin' in schools. Take this screed and break it down a little further, and you'll see it for what it really is: extortion.

These opportunistic NRA-hiney-smoochin' politicians are sayin', "If you give us the prayer in schools we want, we can make all this violence go away, and your kids can be safe." It's probably a little stark and unpopular to say it like that, but that don't make it any less true.

It's simply a process of elimination. They can't blame the gun, because that's their product. They can't blame the shooter, cause that's their market. So all that's left to blame is the victims. You can't advocate bringin' guns into the public square without takin' responsibility for what happens when you do. This ain't called "gun control," it's called bein' a "responsible adult."

On June 17, 2015, Alt-Right white supremacist Dylann Roof walked into the Emanuel African Episcopal Church in Charleston, South Carolina, and killed nine folks includin' the senior pastor. This was right in the middle of a prayer service. If any gun nut had claimed it was because them nine folks weren't prayin' hard enough, they would have had to call a proctologist to have Tea Pain's size 11 boot surgically removed from their hind quarters.

Instead, the NRA did the only logical thing they could think of: blame the victims for not totin' their guns to church. But keep in mind, if they had, they would have got caught up in Trump's "stop and frisk" policy and lost their guns and perished anyway. Dang, schillin' for the NRA is exhaustin'. Maybe that's why politicians that do it get paid so much.

Tea Pain
@TeaPainUSA

Men should enjoy a gun like they enjoy their pornography, in the privacy of their home. Not out in public wavin' it around. #Oathkeepers

Owning guns is totally legal. So is pornography. If it's perfectly acceptable to open carry your assault rifle into Chipotle, it should be perfectly fine to take your notebook full of naughty videos into a Chili's, right? Folks wanna open carry at church, why not open carry an armload of *Hustler* magazines to your house of worship next Sunday mornin'?

Don't get Tea Pain wrong. He's not tryin' to start a #pornsense hashtag or advocate public porn parties at Buffalo Wild Wings. Just the opposite. Guns in public places, businesses and churches are no less distasteful or disruptive as that weird guy in booth number three watchin' "Good Will Humping" too loud on his iPhone.

Now Tea Pain's afraid he's given some idiot the idea of playin' with their gun while they watch pornography at Applebee's. Something's bound to go off and hurt somebody. That would definitely not be "good in the neighborhood."

Tea Pain
@TeaPainUSA

Martyrs shed their blood on the sand in the Coliseum so modern "Christians" can feel persecuted about 30 round magazine legislation. #tcot

You'll forgive Tea Pain if he don't cry any crocodile tears for these poor, "persecuted" Seventh-Day Smith and Wessonites.

Tea Pain
@TeaPainUSA

Trump's 2nd Amendment fanatics say guns are worth dyin' for. But yell "gun" at a Trump rally and watch everybody pee their pants.

12:46 AM - Nov 8, 2016   ♡ 46   ♺ 772   ♡ 1,531

During the heat of Trump's campaign in August 2016, he was warnin' the crowd about the possibility of Hillary gettin' elected and nominatin' Supreme Court justices that would take away everybody's guns. Then he suggested if that happened, his "Second Amendment people" could "do something about that." When outrage ensued, Trump's team assured us he was jokin', cause, after all, what's funnier than callin' for the assassination of your political opponent?

In November, at a rally in Reno, Nevada, Trump found himself starin' down the business end of a karma-matic assault rifle. While Trump whooped up the crowd to a frenzy, one feller raised a sign that simply said, "Republicans Against Trump." Trump's crazed followers tried to tear the sign away unsuccessfully, so someone hollered, "Gun!"

That Second Amendment crowd collectively peed their pants and scattered like quail on the first day of huntin' season. Trump hit the deck and was escorted out by the Secret Service. Ain't it funny, all those patriots were terrified by the idea of somebody actually practicin' their "Second Amendment rights?" It's no coincidence that the same politicians who fight for open carry laws are the first ones to forbid guns in the buildings where they work.

Turns out the feller with the sign got badly beaten, but was let go. Oddly, no one there was upset in the least about his First Amendment rights bein' violated. Oh well, the important thing is that no guns were harmed in the incident.

Tea Pain
@TeaPainUSA

Is it time for Trump to give back all the guns Obama took from folks? Oh wait! Never mind.

4:08 PM - Jan 20, 2017   ◯ 34   ↻ 478   ♡ 1,124

Trump got elected, and a funny thing happened. You'd think a Second Amendment friendly president that encouraged his followers to assassinate his political opponent would be a boon for the gun industry. Now that the dictator Obama was cast down from his gun grabbin' throne, you'd think folks would be buyin' handguns and assault rifles like a fat kid on a funnel cake.

Can you believe it? Gun sales actually went down 21%. Then gun stocks dropped 15% in the first few weeks after Trump was inaugurated. How can you explain such an oddity? Racism, perhaps? Nope, gun sales have dropped during other Republican administrations. Terrorism, maybe? Nope, gun sales show no consistent pattern tied to terror activity. Then how do you explain it? Make yourself comfortable cause Tea Pain's about to preach a little.

In the beginnin', God made man and woman and put them in a beautiful garden to take care of it. Everything was goin' about as good as you could hope. Eve didn't have to nag Adam about pullin' weeds, and Adam didn't have to worry about Eve spendin' all their money on shoes. There was no young'uns to take care of. No utility bills. No car notes. No long borin' corporate meetings. It truly was a paradise. That is, until God decided to upset the applecart, so to speak.

All it took was *one* rule. God said they could eat from any tree in the garden except the Tree of Knowledge. Needless to say, that one tree was all Adam and Eve could think about. We all know the story about how the great serpent, the Father of Lies, twisted the simple words of the law and brought about the end of paradise. The moral of the story? Steer clear of talkin' snakes!

DONT TREAD ON ME

Speak of the devil! Ain't it funny that the Tea Party chose a talkin' snake as their symbol? The NRA hit the jackpot when the Tea Party formed. Them NRA serpent-lobbyists stealthily slithered about their rallies, hissin' and spreadin' rumors that a black feller or a lady in a smart pant-suit was comin' for their guns. Even though public shootings were occurin' at a record pace, these forked-tongued politicians whispered softly into the ears of the unwashed mob that the gun problem could be cured by, you guessed it, buyin' MORE guns.

Just like the serpent in the Bible, a few twisted words caused folks to live and act in fear, and decisions made from fear just create more fear. Folks that are afraid of the unknown search for things to give them control, so they buy a gun. Then they're afraid that one is not enough, so they buy two, then three and on and on.

The modern gun industry is all built on fear and lies. When people are tryin' to scare you into doin' something, look a little closer, cause all they're doin' in pickin' your pocket!

On a side note, in Tea Pain's Bible studies, he ran across a rare apocryphal work with a tiny snippet about Adam and Eve after they were cast out of the garden. When translated from the original Chaldean, it says...

"One day Adam, Eve and their family were passing by the Eastern Gate of the garden of the Lord. Adam said, 'Hey, kids! See that? We used to live there till your Mom ate us outta house and home.'"

- - -

Addicted to Guns
(Robert Palmer Remix)

The lights are on, nobody's home
Tea Party mind, is not your own
The NRA hollows the point
Another gun is what you want

A thirty-eight, a forty-five
Nobody counts innocent lives
Cry bout your rights, while others bleed
Another gun is what you need

So many school shootings we're immune to the stuff
Oh yeah
How many victims till we say it's enough?
You know we're gonna have to face it
We're addicted to guns

8. GAYS

Tea Pain
@TeaPainUSA

@RoundTripp So gay people having equal rights causes folks to "lose their religion?" Sounds like a mighty weak religion to ol' Tea Pain.

There's an ol' sayin': "Your freedom to swing your fist ends where my nose begins." Don't know who wrote that, but he was probably a pretty smart feller. Sounds like a feller that may have been in a scrap or two himself, don't you reckon?

America would be a fine place if folks could just grasp this little nugget of wisdom. Especially when it comes to sexual orientation and marriage.

The above tweet was a question Tea Pain had for this silly feller:

Mike Abramovich @RoundTripp · 5 Apr 2016
@TeaPainUSA I've no problem who gets married.Just don't force people to lose their religion.Isn't religious persecution the reason US formed

Ol' Mikey here has a funny way of lookin' at the world. He thinks since folks like him can't handle gay folks gettin' married, then the *gay folks* must be the problem. Christians boast about the might of their faith and the miracles God has wrought through His faithful believers; that is, until a gay couple moves in next door. Tea Pain's reminded of an ol' joke his daddy used to tell:

There was this feller that called the cops because the neighbors were sunbathin' naked in their backyard. When the cops arrived, they asked which neighbor was doin' it. The man pointed at his neighbor's fence.

"We don't see anything," replied one cop.

"Well, you gotta climb up on the roof first."

You see, that feller had to go to an awful lot of trouble to be offended by his neighbor. If what two consentin' adults do in the privacy of their own home bothers you, *you* just might be the problem.

Tea Pain
@TeaPainUSA

FUN FACT: Craigslist gay encounter listings triple durin' #CPAC week.

1:10 AM - Feb 21, 2017   ♡ 47   ↻ 551   ♡ 1,194

Tea Pain was raised Southern Baptist and preached most every Sunday at the First Baptist Church, but every now and then he'd visit the local Church of Christ just to be neighborly. Church of Christ folks is a lot like Baptists, except they's way more conservative and think every other church is goin' to hell. Other than that, they's some mighty fine folks. The most noticeable difference is that they don't use musical instruments in church, because God never said worship was supposed to be fun. They's the one group in Gizzard Ridge that makes the Baptists look like the "party crowd."

About fifteen years ago, they had this young feller preachin' there that was a mighty good speaker, probably cause he was a drama major from that big swanky Bible college down in Searcy. Funny thing, each time Tea visited, this young man, Lonnie, was always preachin' about Sodom and Gomorrah. Come to think of it, each of the four times Tea Pain visited, Lonnie unleashed a fire-and-brimstone pew-burner about homosexuality. Tea Pain wasn't sure who Pastor Lonnie was workin' harder to convince: himself or the congregation.

Now, Tea Pain ain't a learned feller, but he did see Hamlet once. Remember that part where Queen Gertrude was asked what she thought about the play where the king was poisoned the same way Hamlet's daddy was. She responded "The lady doth protest too much, methinks." That sho nuff seemed to be the situation here as well, and like Hamlet, no one seemed to have caught on as of yet.

Someone once said, "Nature abhors a vacuum," which in the real world probably means that secrets can't stay hidden forever. Such was the case here.

One day a rumor started goin' around Gizzard Ridge that a young assistant minister at the Church of Christ up in Harrison had gotten in a world of trouble, cause he was seen kissin' a feller behind the church a couple of weeks ago after a Bible study. The young minister was placed on suspension, and rumor had it he agreed to undergo counselin'. As soon as Pastor Lonnie heard about it, he eagerly agreed to help the young man that had lost his way.

Even though it was a dark twisty two-lane road to Harrison, Pastor Lonnie made the long drive every night for three weeks straight. Folks were so proud of how their preacher made savin' that poor feller's soul his number one goal in life.

Late one Saturday night, an elder at Pastor Lonnie's church called Tea Pain and asked if Tea could fill in for Pastor Lonnie the followin' morning, provided Tea Pain would preach about anything except Sodom and Gomorrah. Tea Pain was always eager to help a neighborin' church out and gladly accepted.

Turns out Pastor Lonnie and the Harrison minister had mysteriously disappeared. Needless to say, the elders weren't exactly forthcomin' with further details. After a few months of gossipin' and speculatin', the story faded away, and church business went on as usual.

Out of the blue, Tea Pain got a friend request on Facebook about a year ago from Pastor Lonnie. He and that other feller snuck off to Connecticut and got married a few years back . Now they are runnin' a used book shop in Central Florida and raisin' the cutest set of twin Korean boys you ever laid eyes on.

Tea Pain said all that just to say this: true, lastin' love is a mighty rare thing, and it would be a sin to keep it from happenin' between two folks just because they don't match a narrow-minded idea of what a relationship should look like.

Tea Pain
@TeaPainUSA

Jeb Bush says states should determine if gay folks are really humans. #tcot #p2 @JebBush #uniteblue

Every major Civil Rights breakthrough in American history was met with intense resistance from Conservatives. Slavery, Civil Rights, interracial marriage and, finally, gay marriage all faced the same bigoted argument known as "states' rights."

Prior to the Civil War, the Southern slave states argued that the federal government had no power to prohibit or regulate their ownership of slaves, insistin' slave ownership was a matter of "states' rights." Even though Tommy Jefferson said, "All men are created equal," states' righters claim the final say should be left up to, say, South Carolina or Mississippi. It takes a mighty fevered brain to assert that one state can declare a black man a human being and another deem him personal property.

As gay rights advocates struggled to gain the same rights and freedoms as other folks, they were met with the same exact arguments as those who fought to stop interracial marriage. "States' rights" advocates claimed that a state had the right to regulate marriage as they saw fit. You know you're on the right side of history when the other side busts out the same bigoted arguments that didn't work for slavery, Civil Rights or interracial marriage.

 Tea Pain
@TeaPainUSA

If Ted Cruz gets elected gays will have more choices, too! Like which state to move to that will recognize them as human beings.

In virtually every case throughout history, "states' rights" is always diametrically opposed to the rights of minorities. In a nutshell: scratch a "states' rights" fan and you'll find a bigot every time.

 Tea Pain
@TeaPainUSA

If you want to...
1. Ban Islam
2. Ban a women's choice
3. Ban Gay Marriage
...you might not be for smaller gubment. #tcot

When you run into a Tea Partier fussin' about "big gubment," chances are all you've found is a feller that don't like payin' taxes. They preach about fewer laws and more freedom, but, truth be told, that's absolutely the last thing they want. What they really want is a powerful, authoritarian government with more laws that take away freedom from folks they don't like.

These irony-impaired cosplay "patriots" wave the Constitution in one hand and the Rebel flag in the other. They stand on their little soapboxes and speechify about how all men are created equal and how freedom and liberty should ring throughout the land. Then they trot out their little list of exceptions.

First, they'll tell you America is all about religious freedom and how the foundin' fathers insured us we can all worship in the manner of our choosin', with the small exception, of course, of Muslims. As a matter of fact, they'll tell you the Constitution is sadly lackin' an amendment about bannin' Islam from our shores. They claim no watchful patriot should abide a religious group that is "ruinin' this country with their radical, extremist ideology."

Don't get 'em started on women's rights. Accordin' to them, there's a whole bunch of new laws that need to be passed to keep all them "godless Liberals from murderin' babies," even though over three-fourths of the women that get abortions identify as Christian.

Lastly comes the big ticket item: gay marriage! Even after the Supreme Court ruled that gay marriage was the law of the land, folks like Ted Cruz and his hoard of homophobes called for a Constitutional amendment to outlaw gay marriage. More laws to take away more freedoms ain't equality, friends. It's fascism.

The real kick in the pants? These God-fearin' Christians have identical positions on gay marriage, guns, abortion and women's rights as the Muslims who they say are "ruinin' this country with their radical, extremist ideologies."

Tea Pain
@TeaPainUSA

Conservatives don't want gay marriage to ruin the sanctity of Christian divorce. #tcot #ccot #marriageeqaulity

No doubt the silliest argument against gay marriage is that it "ruins the sanctity of Christian marriage." For the past 25 years, two out of every three heterosexual marriages have ended in divorce. You can surely see why they don't want gay folks to come in and ruin all that sanctity!

Another fun fact: Jesus never personally commented on homosexuality, but he did talk about divorce. "Anyone who divorces his wife and marries another woman commits adultery, and the man who marries a divorced woman commits adultery." - Luke 16:18.

It's mighty convenient that Jesus is more than willin' to overlook our record-settin' pace on divorce, but has a zero-tolerance policy when it comes to the gay stuff.

Tea Pain
@TeaPainUSA

Turns out Christian Divorce can be blamed on gay marriage instead of epidemic adultery as first suspected. #TeaBomb

"Everybody knows that God controls weather," said Susanne Atanus, GOP nominee for Illinois's 9th district. "God is super angry. Gay marriage is not appropriate, and it doesn't look right, and it breeds AIDS." Sister Susanne didn't stop there. She also gave gay folks the credit for autism and dementia.

Leadin' science advocate Rick Santorum one-upped ol' Susanne. "Gay marriage doesn't just cause singular events like tornados and terrorism. *It can also cause recessions.*" Predictably, he didn't blame the 2008 recession on near-non-existent bankin' policies or coked-up Wall Street wolverines, but on the "erosion of society" caused by gay marriage. Nothin' gets ol' Rick breathin' heavy and frothin' at the mouth like the image of gay men havin' sex with one another.

If you want something done right, hire a professional. The best gay basher to ever walk the face of ol' Terra Firma was, without a doubt, Jerry Falwell. Remember how those Saudi hijackers knocked down the Twin Towers on 9/11 in the deadliest terrorist attack on American soil? Was it due to Middle East retaliation for decades of invasive American policies? Nope. Was it the beginnings of a pre-apocalyptic Islamist Jihad? No sir! You guessed it: according to Jerry, it was them danged gays' and lesbians' fault!

"I really believe that the pagans, and the abortionists, and the feminists, and the gays and the lesbians who are actively trying to make that an alternative lifestyle - I point the finger in their face and say 'you helped this happen,'" Falwell said.

Let this sink in for a second. Accordin' to Christian phonies like Falwell, God the Father, in his infinite wisdom and boundless mercy, chose to kill 3,000 innocent folks on 9/11 because He saw Larry and Steve pickin' out bric-a-brac at Restoration Hardware? Or maybe the Lord beheld Jenny pickin' up Paula on their second date in a U-Haul truck and was so moved to wrath He flew jet planes into buildings 2,000 miles away?

All Tea Pain's gonna say about that is if you had a father that behaved that reckless and immaturely, you'd have been picked up by child protective services years ago.

Tea Pain
@TeaPainUSA

The families of the victims of the #ColoradoSpringsShooting will find great solace in Ted Cruz tryin' to blame it on the gays.

Ted Cruz took the cake when he claimed Robert Lewis Dear, the lunatic who shot up the Colorado Springs Planned Parenthood facility in 2015, was actually born a woman. This was due to an error by a county clerk that had accidentally marked "female" on Deer's voter registration form. Relyin' on a widely debunked, fake news story genned up by the Internet press-cess-pool known as Gateway Pundit, Ted called this bushy little critter a "transgendered leftist activist" and gladly laid the blame for the horrible tragedy on the LGBTQ doorstep.

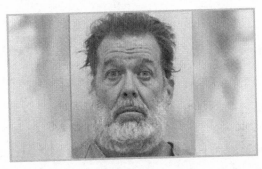

You see, there isn't a single bad thing that happens in America that can't be blamed on gay marriage. All any half-wit politician has to do is sprinkle a little of this magic fairy dust on a tragedy and... boomity bang! Instant gay-tastrophe

All these political shenanigans were welcome news for Christians that for years had blamed themselves for their failed marriages. Turns out it wasn't their fault they cheated on their wife or ran off and left their kids; their decisions and behaviors were only because of them fruity Liberals up in Connecticut gettin' gay married!

Tea Pain @TeaPainUSA · 27 Jun 2015
Bryan is worried less about the **gay** man on the street and more about the **gay** man inside him. @BryanJFischer

Bryan Fischer
@BryanJFischer

They've got sodomy-based marriage. Now they must hunt down and destroy any who defend natural marriage. It's gonna get ugly.

Speakin' of ladies that "doth protest too much," meet Bryan Fischer. He's a nutball talker on American Family Radio. You might say Bryan went into his "prayer closet" one day and has yet to come out.

Even though only 3.8% of the U.S. population is gay, Bryan paints a picture of an America overrun by the "Gaystapo" with gays roamin' the streets night and day and holdin' giant Nuremberg-sized rallies. One minute, gays are effeminate pajama-boys seekin' out little kids to molest; the next they are violent Spartans huntin' in packs, seekin' out happily married straight couples to gun down while the Gaypocalypse end-times rage.

Funny thing, Bryan talks about gay men more than actual gay men do. In his warped version of history, even Hitler and all the Nazis were gay. Come to think of it, everywhere Bryan looks, he sees gay men; sweaty, chiseled, muscular, assless-chaps-wearin' gay men.

Tea Pain's gonna share a pro tip with you. When you see fellers like Bryan and them other anti-gay militants ragin' on about homosexuality, read their statements real careful. If they sound less like political commentary and more like personal fantasy, then there ya go!

On a personal note: Tea Pain's lived a long time and never had one problem with any gay folks ever. But in Tea Pain's circle of family and friends, three women have been sexually attacked by straight men. In all three cases, the attacks were from Baptist ministers.

Tea's wept when he's read stories in the paper about little kids bein' molested in church-run daycare centers by actual members of the church. A few years back, Tea Pain heard about a youth minister in Memphis arrested for runnin' a child pornography network. Folks like Bryan Fischer might wanna actually read the Bible a little, then clean up their own backyard before they cast stones at gay folks.

It's Tea's opinion that folks like Bryan never truly answered Jesus' call: "Follow me, and I will make you fishers of men," mainly because it just sounded "too gay."

- - -

Independence Gay
(Martina McBride Remix)

Conservatives cried all day last Friday
When SCOTUS said gay marriage was cool
Hannity gripped for the Gay-pocalypse
As the folks at Fox began to drool
Twitter caught fire like a funeral pyre
A Facebook was a hate buffet
Talkin' bout Obamanation
It's Independence Gay

Let the church bells ring
And let Cher sing
And let the U.S. know it's okay for gay weddings
Let the Left be strong, cause the Right is wrong
Let's get hitched today, nothings in our way,
Independence Gay

9. MASTER DEBATERS

Tea Pain
@TeaPainUSA

1000 white folks and 1 black feller? It's either the #GOPDebate or a KKK meetin'. #TeaLiveTweets

When you scan the crowd at a GOP debate, you are immediately struck by the amount of diversity. There's white Southern Baptists, white Presbyterians, white Methodists and white Evangelicals. Heck, they even peppered in a few white Catholics just to show off!

You see, the GOP is all about diversity. They don't care which part of Northern Europe your folks came from.

Tea Pain
@TeaPainUSA

All four candidates say God called them to run. Looks like God's playin' a prank on at least three of 'em. #GOPDebate #TeaTweets

As a student of the Scriptures, Tea Pain has never understood how anybody can think the good Lord gives a hoot about politics. Jesus was put to death by Pontius Pilate, a Roman politician. The disciples were persecuted by politicians and government officials all over the Roman Empire. Jesus was clear on the matter, "My kingdom is not of this world." So anybody that thinks God has a dog in the hunt when it comes to politics is crazier than a bag full of bobcats.

In 2016, four of the GOP candidates declared that "God had told them to run for president." Walker, Cruz, Carson and Huckabee all proclaimed that God Almighty instructed them to throw their tin-foil hats into the ring.

Tea Pain don't doubt for a minute that Mike Huckabee hears voices, just not from the benevolent Creator of the universe. Ben Carson most likely dreamed God spoke to him durin' one of his famous "power naps." But when it comes to Cruz and Walker, multiple sources confirm that Jesus's daddy has both of them scoundrels on the "Do Not Call" list.

Tea Pain
@TeaPainUSA

Trump: "The dishonest media is constantly attacking me by replaying audio and video of all the things I say and do. VERY SAD!"

12:04 PM - Jan 9, 2017   ♡ 113   ⟲ 1,784   ♡ 3,212

Turns out the real problem in America is all them educated folks with their snooty complete sentences and their biased television cameras askin' "gotcha" questions and recordin' your answers.

Tea Pain
@TeaPainUSA

Tonight, the GOP candidates proclaimed Trump unfit for office. Then they all promised to support him. #TrueStory #TeaTweets

11:47 PM - Mar 3, 2016   🗨 14   ↻ 164   ♡ 169

Durin' the debates and the primaries, the other GOP candidates had mighty interestin' things to say about Donald Trump. Ted Cruz called him a "narcissist" and a "pathological liar." Jeb Bush called him a "loser" and a "whiner." John Kasich said he is "divisive" and compared him to Adolf Hitler. Marco Rubio said he was a "con-man" and "not prepared to be Commander-in-Chief."

When it appeared that Trump was most likely gonna be the nominee, the other candidates were asked if they would support him. It went down something like this:

Moderator: Do you believe Mr. Trump is dangerous and unstable?
Candidates: Yes
Moderator: Do you agree Mr. Trump is a pathological liar?
Candidates: Yes
Moderator: Do you believe Mr. Trump is unfit to serve?
Candidates: Yes
Moderator: Is he a cancer on our democracy?
Candidates: Yes!
Moderator: If Mr. Trump is nominated, will you support him?
Candidates: Absolutely, 100%.

Tea Pain's gonna break down the 2016 presidential field for ya. Here we go!

Scott Walker

Tea Pain
@TeaPainUSA

Scott Walker can't stand Unions. The good news for him is he don't have to worry bout givin' a State of the Union address. #GOPDebate
8:45 PM - Sep 16, 2015

♡ 1   ↻ 34   ♡ 90

Scott Walker believes the best way to improve our education system is to take away benefits from teachers. If you think the biggest problem in America is that our teachers have it too good, don't be surprised when your kid asks you how they get the deer to cross at them yeller road signs.

Walker was a big disappointment for the Koch brothers and the GOP establishment. He was a total no-show in the debates. In fairness to Scott, it's hard to practice debate prep in the mirror when you can't see your own reflection.

Jeb Bush

Tea Pain
@TeaPainUSA

If Democrats waste hundreds of millions of dollars, it's called "socialism". When Republicans do it, it's called the Jeb Bush campaign.
12:50 AM - Feb 21, 2016   ♡ 27   ↻ 350   ♡ 487

Tea Pain
@TeaPainUSA

Every time a bell rings, an angel gets his wings....plus Jeb
Bush's campaigns spends 2 million dollars. #TeaLiveTweets

What Tea Pain never understood was why Christian Conservatives
didn't flock to ol' Jeb, since they get all excited about talkin'
bushes. Seems like the more money ol' Jeb spent, the less excited
folks got about him. In all, Jeb spent over 150 million dollars with
nothin' to show for it. The moral lesson here is that Jeb can spend
all the money he wants, but when it's all over, he's still George
Dubya's brother.

Tea Pain
@TeaPainUSA

Jeb Bush is right. We were attacked and his brother kept us
safe, unless you count the thousands of actual deaths.
#JebBush2016

On live television, ol' Jeb actually bragged about how his brother
Dubya "kept us safe," and how he'd do the same. Maybe Jeb was
right, give or take three thousand folks.

Tea Pain
@TeaPainUSA

Jeb Bush admits he'd kill #BabyHitler but never abort
#FetusHitler.

This is just more proof that Conservatives care about babies till
they're born; then it's every toddler for himself. The way
Republicans see it: they take care of babies for nine months; after
that, they're the Liberals' problem.

Donald Trump

Tea Pain
@TeaPainUSA

Donald Trump knows a lot about Trade. Every 10 years he trades his wife in for a younger model. #TeaTweets

Have you ever wondered how Trump became the darlin' of the Religious Right over bona-fide Evangelicals like Ted Cruz and Mike Huckabee? It's easy; most Evangelicals don't know the Bible from a backhoe. If they actually read it, they'd be Liberals. All they seem to know about Jesus is that He wants a strong military, loves the Second Amendment and looks down on poor folks that are dependent on big government. Oh, and the gays. Jesus hates the gays.

Of all the candidates that the party of "family values" had to choose from, they did the logical thing and chose the feller that had the most families. They never blinked an eye at Trump's three marriages and almost seem to take comfort in his womanizin'. Trump ended up provin' that a man will treat his country the same way he treats a woman.

Tea Pain
@TeaPainUSA

Donald Trump want's every American to ask themselves one question: "Are you better off than you were two marriages ago?" #TeaTweets

When the Hollywood Access tape hit, Liberals wrote Trump off, cause they didn't think anybody in their right mind would vote for Trump after all that shameful locker room talk he made about lady parts and how fond he is of grabbin' 'em, whether he's invited to or not. Trump's followers failed to see what the big brou-hoo-ha was all about. If anything, they were actually excited about votin' for the "p-grabber-in-chief." No one could accuse Donald's followers of pussy-footin' around, no sir. They literally came outta the bushes to vote and give their private-grabbin' prophet a come-from-behind victory.

> **Tea Pain**
> @TeaPainUSA
>
> Trump doesn't wanna be president for the power, he just likes the idea of kickin' a black family outta their home. #TeaTweets

Donald Trump ran for the highest office in the land with one simple agenda: undo everything done by America's first black president. It was probably Trump's delayed reaction to President Obama layin' a top-rope smackdown on him at the White House correspondent's dinner. Or it might have been due to the dirty trick Obama pulled on Trump by bein' born in America and havin' a birth certificate.

Ted Cruz

> **Tea Pain**
> @TeaPainUSA
>
> Ted Cruz will remove all education standards on day one, essentially turnin' us all into Republicans. #GOPDebates #TeaTweets

What is it that makes Republicans hate education so much? A recent poll showed that 54% of Republicans think college is a "bad thing."

In the days of Ronald Reagan, the American dream included a college education, a good job and a happy family. Under the new GOP, the Holy Grail of success in life is to own your own liquor store.

Tea Pain
@TeaPainUSA

Ted Cruz is complainin' they ain't askin' the questions he practiced answerin' in front of a mirror all day. #GOPDebate #CruzCrew #Cruz2016

At Harvard, Ted Cruz was voted "most likely to die at the hands of his dormmates." Ted actually leaves strategic pauses in his speeches to allow for prolonged laughter and applause.

Tea Pain
@TeaPainUSA

Ted Cruz: "Washington DC is the problem. I know. I work there." #GOPDebate

There's an old sayin' in politics: "Every election, Republicans tell us the 'government is broken.' Then we send 'em to Washington, and they prove it." Only Ted Cruz is brazen enough to blame D.C. for our problems while he's a sittin' U.S. Senator.

Tea Pain
@TeaPainUSA

Ted Cruz is still endorsing' Donald Trump because racism and sexual assault don't conflict with Ted's Christian values.
12:19 AM - Oct 11, 2016   ♡ 70   ⟲ 885   ♡ 1,398

2016 was the year that "Conservative Christians" decided to forgive every sin in the book, with the exception of bein' born black or a woman. Ted Cruz never once spoke out against Trump's Alt-Right white supremacy movement or his sexual assaults on women. Once you stopped blowin' on the fur and got to the hide, Cruz's biggest problem with Trump was that he was a better liar than Ted. In other words: *professional jealousy.*

Ben Carson

Tea Pain
@TeaPainUSA

Most reasonable feller in the room tonight claims a black president is like Hitler and Health Insurance is worse than slavery. #TeaTweets

9:19 PM - Feb 25, 2016   💬   ↻ 22   ♡ 25

One of the most memorable "Carsonisms" was when he said that "Obamacare was worse than slavery." Ben said this, innocuous to the irony that his party would be more than willin' to put black folks back in chains to save 'em from the horrors of havin' affordable health insurance.

Tea Pain
@TeaPainUSA

Ben Carson: "I'm the only person here to remove half a brain."

Mike Huckabee: "And I didn't feel a thing!"#GOPDebate

10:02 PM - Aug 6, 2015   💬 26   ↻ 423   ♡ 532

It must have been so frustratin' for Ben to know the one thing standin' between him and the presidency was the one brain he couldn't operate on.

Marco Rubio

Tea Pain
@TeaPainUSA

Marco Rubio said he might have done better if he hadn't been accused of bein' a robot. Then he paused to download an update.

Marco Rubio just couldn't get it goin' in the 2016 presidential race, despite rebootin' his campaign twice and himself four times. Turns out the problem was they were both runnin' on Windows Vista. Marco 2.0 got caught in a program loop and repeated the same script word-for-word four times durin' one of the debates. This was the end-of-file for little Marco.

The good news is that Marco Rubio is young and "may run again one day," provided his firmware will support the latest version of Windows.

> **Tea Pain**
> @TeaPainUSA
>
> Marco Rubio best represents the average American. Note the average American didn't win any delegates yesterday, either.

The American people dodged a bullet in 2016. If Kim Jong Un had figured out a way to mount the Rubio campaign on one of his missiles, America would have been doomed. In fairness to Marco, he's a decent feller and a lot of folks identified with him as an "average American." Sadly for Rubio, the "average American" didn't have a prayer either.

John Kasich

> **Tea Pain**
> @TeaPainUSA
>
> John Kasich seems likable, reasonable and thoughtful and that's why he don't stand a chance. #GOPDebate
> 8:35 PM - Aug 6, 2015   ○ 26   ↻ 252   ♡ 401

John Kasich was the most seasoned and polished candidate in the GOP field. He was level-headed, well-spoken, thoughtful and reasonable. He kept his cool while all the other Republicans were behavin' like a buncha drunk monkeys. He was smart, mature and would have made a steady Commander-in-Chief. In other words: the feller never stood a chance.

It seemed the highest priority among Republican voters in 2016 was that their candidate must have appeared on at least two episodes of WWE Smackdown.

Mike Huckabee

Tea Pain
@TeaPainUSA

Huckabee just sewed up the 75 and older vote with the Buick abortion riff! #GOPDebate

Mike Huckabee has two main criteria for his jokes. First, they must be based on widely debunked InfoWars memes and, second, they are never to be accompanied by any actual laughter. Despite evidence to the contrary, Huck fancied himself the next Mark Twain and was confident he would separate himself from the pack with his folksy, man-of-the-people banter. He just needed the right moment.

That moment came on live television with millions of undecided voters watchin'. The scene was set. The moderator had just lobbed him a softball, a big sweet hangin' curveball about abortion. Seizin' the moment, Huck uncoiled like a rattlesnake and swung for the fences. "Planned Parenthood is in the business of selling babies' body parts like the parts of a Buick."

Huck flashed a smile of proud accomplishment and waited for the laughter to erupt and wash over him like the Holy Ghost at a tent revival'… but the laughter never came. Turns out, old white folks love their Buicks. Dang Republicans, way to leave a brother hangin'!

Mike Huckabee has a God-given talent of pickin' the worst possible analogies to explain things. He once tweeted that "kids

should get off their butts and serve their country." Funny, since he
never served in the military himself. Guess ol' Huck was bettin'
those kids wouldn't "get off their butts" and Google his military
record.

Tea Pain
@TeaPainUSA

Huckabee on Iran Deal: "Ronald Reagan said 'Trust, but
verify.', then he sold weapons to 'em anyway." #GOPDebate

Invokin' the ghost of Ronald Reagan to address the Iran nuclear
deal is like askin' O.J. Simpson to host a seminar against domestic
violence.

Reagan actually sold missiles to Iran while they were under a U.S.
arms embargo, then sent the money to Manuel Noriega to finance
a revolution in Nicaragua. George Dubya's daddy had to pardon
six of Reagan's co-conspirators involved in the scandal that plagued
Reagan's second term. What regular folks call "criminal,"
Republicans call "presidential."

Chris Christie

Tea Pain
@TeaPainUSA

Chris Christie promised Hillary Clinton won't get within 10
miles of the White House. Did he just vow to block another
bridge? #GOPDebate

Poor Chris Christie. He planned for years to be the next president
by bein' a populist, loudmouth, narcissistic bully. Sadly, his plans
were doused by a populist, loudmouth, narcissistic bully with a
reality show.

After he suspended his campaign, the press asked Christie what his plans were for the future. Christie responded, "I don't know; I'll block that bridge when I get to it."

After Trump was elected, Christie announced he was "not interested in a job in the White House," which worked out great, since no one had asked.

- - -

Master Debaters

Trump the Trump, yeah, Fox put the hit out
Went after Donald before he got his mitts out
The Fox Panel was steamin' like a boiler
Prayin' that the Donald's not a third-party spoiler

Christie and Rand weren't actin' like old gumbas
Any more tension and they'd have to get a room-ba

John Kasich gave clear and thoughtful answers
Poor ol' feller he doesn't stand a chance-a.

Scott Walker he went missin' and Cruz looked like a vampire
While Jebbie Bush was dancin' puttin' out his brother's wildfire

Bennie Carson told us he took out half a brain
Mike Huckabee bragged that he didn't feel a thing.

10. TRUMP VS. OBAMA

Tea Pain
@TeaPainUSA

FUN FACT: All the Boy Scouts that attended Trump's jamboree speech just earned a merit badge for workin' with the mentally disabled.
11:08 PM - Jul 24, 2017 ♡ 406 ⟲ 4,356 ♡ 12,730

Of all the crazy things Trump has done as president, perhaps the most tellin' thing was when he addressed the National Boy Scout Jamboree in July 2017. Trump did his dead-level best in 30 minutes to transform a group of fine, upstandin' boys into his own personal Twitler Youth.

Trump kicked off his speech, "Who the hell wants to speak about politics when I'm in front of the Boy Scouts? Right?" The boys cheered wildly, but then Trump proceeded to do precisely what he just said he wouldn't.

The first lesson he taught the boys was respect for the office of the president. He taunted President Obama for not showin' up to the previous Jamboree four years ago, even though Mr. Obama had sent a special video message. He actually pushed the boys to boo the first black president of the United States for bein' too lazy to show up, even though Obama was actually a member of the Scouts as a boy and Trump wasn't. He wanted the boys to know it's very important to back the white, er, right president.

Next, Trump began recitin' the Boy Scout pledge... about how a scout must be "trustworthy and loyal," commentin' that "We could use some more loyalty, I will tell you that." He said this on the same day he was sendin' out tweet after tweet assaultin' his own Attorney General, Jeff Sessions - his earliest Senate endorser - simply for follerin' the law and recusin' himself from the criminal investigation against Trump.

Always obsessed with size, Trump then claimed the crowd was "record-setting," at least 45,000, however the actual crowd size was less than half that. Trump couldn't help but to pretend that his captive audience of adolescent boys was actually a campaign rally.

Trump really connected with the young crowd by addressin' the one thing every teenage boy lays in bed at night and fantasizes about: *health insurance*. Trump gave no real details, but he assured everyone that his administration was working hard on "killing this horrible thing known as Obamacare that's really hurting us."

The message received? "Remember that black feller we booed a minute ago? He's tryin' to kill us all!"

Trump then lept into a morality play about William Levitt, a millionaire New York real estate developer that sold his company, bought a yacht and led a "very interesting life," referrin' to Levitt's infamous cocaine-fueled at-sea orgies with underage girls. Trump's suggestive and titillatin' message only piqued the young boys' interests, so any dutiful Scout that later researched Levitt's life would not only find out about his statutory peccadillos, but also learn he was notorious for not sellin' properties to black folks. The score at the end of the speech: Caucasians 3, Minorities 0.

The next day the White House physician had to be called in to treat the president for minor sprains from pattin' himself on the back. To combat the unanimously negative reviews of his ramblin' shenanigans, Trump spun up a tale claimin' the head of the Boy

Scouts called to thank him for deliverin' the "greatest speech ever given," even though no BSA official was aware of such a phone call ever takin' place. A few days later, a real Scout official apologized for Trump's "incendiary political rhetoric." On the upside, all the Boy Scouts earned a merit badge for learnin' how to build a dumpster fire with a single teleprompter.

Tea Pain
@TeaPainUSA

Trump questions why President Obama don't get accused of sexual assault. Probably because he don't sexually assault women.

7:27 PM - Oct 14, 2016   ⏺ 38   ⏹ 337   ♡ 757

Trump actually believed he could deflect from his self-confessed womanizin' by challengin' the press as to why President Obama never got accused of assaultin' women. Turns out it was the same reason why Mother Teresa was never accused of murder: cause she never actually murdered anybody. President Obama was the model of a strong family man who loved his wife and kids and treated women with kindness and respect. This was the first great Obama era policy Trump ended on day one.

Tea Pain
@TeaPainUSA

Trump says Obama's lettin' immigrants "pour into this country to vote", instead of makin' teen models out of 'em, like Jesus commanded.

10:58 AM - Oct 7, 2016   ♡ 18   ↻ 393   ♡ 783

Trump just praised Obama for deportin' millions of illegals, while claimin' Obama's importin' millions of illegals to vote against him.

8:33 PM - Oct 19, 2016   ♡ 22   ↻ 270   ♡ 436

Why have something one way, when you can have it both ways? Donnie "Two Scoops" was the king of contradictions, which ain't that big a deal when you consider his supporters have the attention span of a mosquito on crystal meth.

On October 7th, 2016, he criticized the president for allowin' illegals to "pour into this country to vote." The fact that illegals can't vote is beside the point and only detracts from Trump's story about how Mexicans are to blame for pretty much everything. Now, don't read Trump the wrong way. He ain't opposed to all immigration. As a matter of fact, he throws America's gates open wide to young, thin, hot, former Soviet bloc models, preferably under 18.

Less than two weeks later, after his immigration plan was called "cruel and inhumane," because it would break up families and even deport Dreamers, Trump pointed out the real deporter-in-chief was President Obama. He then turned and actually praised Obama for deportin' so many folks. So take note: the only time Trump ever said anything positive about the first black president was when he was deportin' brown-skinned folks. Trump is an "ass-half-full" kinda guy.

Tea Pain
@TeaPainUSA

If Obama hadn't allowed the Khan's to come to America in 1980, then Trump wouldn't have had to attack their family. #KatrinaPiersonHistory

Remember when Trump attacked the Khans, a gold-star Muslim family whose only crime was speakin' out against Trump's proposed Muslim ban? The entire nation collectively gasped as Trump lit into the Khans, especially since they had recently lost their beloved son in the service of our great nation. Trump's biggest attack was based on the fact that Mrs. Khan didn't speak, as if Mr. Khan had forbidden her or perhaps dark forces from Muslim headquarters were at work. We later learned that Mrs. Khan couldn't even be in the same room with her son's pictures without cryin' and breakin' down.

Needless to say, the reviews of Trump's Khan-tastrophe weren't good, so team Trump called out the top shelf nutballs to go on TV and fix it. One of Trump's primo wackadoos was Katrina Pierson, who went on CNN and, with a straight face, claimed that it was all Obama's fault for lettin' the Khans into the country in the first place. Her logic was unassailable, because if the Khans weren't here, then it would have been impossible for Trump to have been "tricked" into attackin' 'em.

Katrina's revisionist history lesson was wolfed down like gravy on a biscuit by Trump's basket full of irony-impaired deplorables. Turns out the Khans came to America in 1980, 28 years before Obama was elected, but Professor Pierson assured us that dates wouldn't be on the test. If it were December, perhaps Hurricane Katrina might have churned up a Cat-5 whopper about how Obama attacked Pearl Harbor.

Tea Pain
@TeaPainUSA

Rudy Giuliani says Trump "now believes Obama was born in the U.S.", probably because Trump just learned Hawaii is not part of Kenya.

9:40 PM - Sep 8, 2016   ○ 28   ↻ 294   ♡ 563

Speakin' of Hawaii, did you know Obama was born there? Trump spent five years promotin' one of the vilest, most racist screeds in political history. Accordin' to Trump and the far-right, there must be a sinister reason that America had elected its first black president. Seriously, there's no way a black man could obtain such an achievement without deceit and chicanery or, at the very worst, not without the help of rich, white benefactors, right?

The "Birther Movement" proved that racism was alive, well and thrivin' deep in the base of the Republican party, and no one fanned the racist flames more effectively than Donald Trump. Remember these juicy Trump tweets?

Donald J. Trump ✓
@realDonaldTrump

An 'extremely credible source' has called my office and told me that @BarackObama's birth certificate is a fraud.

3:23 PM - Aug 6, 2012

And...

Donald J. Trump ✓
@realDonaldTrump

Wake Up America! See article: "Israeli Science: Obama Birth Certificate is a Fake"

10:40 AM - Sep 13, 2012

Trump was already a Tea Party hero for hangin' ten on this gnarly wave of thinly-veiled racism. Bustin' out the "Mexicans are rapists" riff in Phoenix elevated Trump to the de facto Grand Wizard of the Tea Party. This Molotov cocktail of hate exploded into a mushroom cloud that launched Trump all the way to the GOP party nomination. But, as the general election drew near, Trump was faced with a decision that was sho nuff hard to make. The establishment wing of the Republican party was ridin' him hard to denounce "birtherism" due to daily accusations of racism from the left that plagued his flaggin' campaign.

You gotta hand it to Trump. He found a way out that was borderline genius. Since he couldn't blame the birther movement on Obama, he blamed it on Hillary. First rule of Trumpism: "If you can't blame a minority, blame a woman!"

How did we "Nazi" this comin'? Trump's racism wasn't his fault. It was Hillary's!

Tea Pain
@TeaPainUSA

Trump folks is still complainin' about President Obama's use of a teleprompter cause it's a sore reminder he can read.

3:11 PM - Jul 29, 2016   ♡ 19   ⟳ 102   ♡ 263

Trump's clan claimed Obama wasn't a legitimate president because he used a teleprompter. They claim he used it cause he was actually stupid and that Harvard had faked his scholarships and hid his grades because, you know, black folks can't achieve anything on their own.

Tea Pain
@TeaPainUSA

GOP 2008: Obama's not Presidential. Anyone can read off a teleprompter.
GOP 2017: Trump read a speech off a teleprompter! So Presidential!

9:44 AM - Mar 1, 2017 　　152　　3,026　　4,889

After a disastrous start to his presidency, Trump's staff sat on his chest long enough to convince him to read a speech from a teleprompter. They proclaimed it the "greatest speech in presidential history" simply because Trump didn't throw up on national television. Ain't it sad that a white man "became president" that night for barely clearin' the same bar they belittled a black man for?

Tea Pain
@TeaPainUSA

Last night President Obama painted a future of love, hope and unity, while Donald Trump recounted 39 ways we can be murdered in our sleep.

7:33 AM - Jul 28, 2016　　5　　153　　266

Obama inspired millions of kids to pursue public service due to his own personal success story. He was livin' proof that any kid - red, yellow, black or white - could grow up to be the leader of the free world.

Trump on the other hand believed America was a swelterin' cesspool of failure; a place where no one could walk down the street without their throat bein' slit by an inner-city drug lord or their women raped by roamin' gangs of illegal Mexicans. Even Rick Grimes would be no match for the post-Obama apocalyptic landscape Trump painted. By Trump's reckonin', the lucky souls would be the ones murdered in their sleep by ISIS and spared the flamin' carnage that was America.

Tea Pain
@TeaPainUSA

Name 3 terrorist groups.

Obama: "ISIS, Hezbollah and Hamas"

Trump: "CNN, Saturday Night Live and the New York Times"

4:57 PM - Dec 6, 2016   ♡ 55   ↻ 1,012   ♡ 1,613

As of the writing of this book, it's six months into Trump's presidency. He promised to have a plan to defeat ISIS in 30 days, yet we ain't seen hide nor hair of any plan yet. But Trump has had time to play 53 rounds of golf and launch Twitter wars against Nordstrom, CNN, Saturday Night Live, the New York Times and the Washington Post.

Tea Pain
@TeaPainUSA

Trump wants us to believe Obama tapped his phones, but forgot to leak his tax returns. #TrumpRussia

5:55 PM - Mar 5, 2017   ♡ 142   ↻ 4,052   ♡ 7,610

Even though Trump despised everything President Obama stood for and his entire platform was built on tearin' down every great thing Mr. Obama did for our country, Trump did find Obama to be mighty handy to have around to blame his own personal failures on.

In the early days of the Russia scandal, Trump was able to simply dismiss it as a hoax. But shortly after his inauguration, it came out that the intelligence agencies had intercepts of National Security Advisor Mike Flynn discussin' liftin' sanctions with the Russian ambassador. Seein' no other way around it, Trump did the only sensible thing he could: blame Obama.

Turns out, according to Trump, Obama had violated dozens of laws and had Trump Tower illegally tapped to monitor his every phone call. Havin' zero proof of such heinous crimes actually bein' committed didn't slow Trump down one bit. He just kept tweetin' up a storm about all the horrible things that naughty Obama had done to poor innocent Donald. Some of his minions even started a rumor that Obama had stolen Trump's tax returns.

Tea Pain
@TeaPainUSA

Press: 17 intel agencies all agree.

GOP: We see no evidence of Russian involvement.

Trump: Obama tapped me!

GOP: We'll get right on it!

1:52 PM - Mar 5, 2017   💬 92   🔁 2,254   ♡ 3,650

The Republicans proved they would go to the ends of the Earth to protect their plump orange messiah. Despite a unanimous consensus from every U.S. intelligence agency that Russia interfered in our election, they just couldn't see it. But the minute Donald tweeted that a black feller had "tapped" his phones, they started stumblin' all over themselves to investigate. Nothin' gets a bunch of ol' white fellers cranked up like a chance to blame a black feller for their problems.

But if blamin' one black person is good, then blamin' two is even better. So Trump tweeted up a new tale that Susan Rice had broken the law by "unmaskin'" members of his election campaign. His white nationalist base went apey and actually believed that Trump was gonna slap the handcuffs on that ol' criminal Obama hisself!

There was just one little problem with Trump's elaborate yarn: If Obama had all these naughty secrets, as well as his tax returns, why did he never release 'em?

Tea Pain
@TeaPainUSA

Just to reset, Trump's latest version of the Russia story is "Obama is a very bad person for letting me get elected." #TrumpRussia

8:47 AM - Jun 27, 2017   💬 138   🔁 2,284   ♡ 4,587

Seein' the walls closin' in, Trump became more and more desperate is his Russia tweetin'. With every tweet, he made less and less sense about the Russia scandal. By now it was crystal clear that Russia had interfered, so it must be time to blame the black guy once more.

Donald J. Trump ✔ @realDonaldTrump · Jun 23
Just out: The **Obama** Administration knew far in advance of November 8th about election meddling by Russia. **Did nothing** about it. WHY?

So, here's the "logic" behind Trump's argument: Obama knew the Russians were meddlin' with the election four months before election day. Obama knew the Russians were colludin' with Trump to beat Hillary. Obama didn't do anything to stop it; therefore, it's Obama's fault Trump committed treason and became president. Thanks, Obama!

Tea Pain
@TeaPainUSA

After watchin' @PressSec's press conference, near as we can tell, Trump is sayin' Mike Flynn is Obama's fault. #trumprussia

2:22 PM - Apr 25, 2017   💬 202   🔁 1,115   ♡ 2,451

Wait! It gets better. Mike Flynn had been a naughty, naughty boy, talkin' to Russians about liftin' sanctions, workin' secretly as a foreign agent for Turkey and even plottin' to kidnap folks. Trump had picked Flynn as his closest advisor early in his campaign. Flynn stuck by him through thick and thin; they had seen it all and been through it all together. So, when Flynn was caught with his pantaloons down, Trump took full responsibility, right?

Tea Pain
@TeaPainUSA

Trump called Obama's birth certificate "one of the great cons in the history of politics", but never questioned Obama's "vetting" of Flynn?

2:41 PM - Apr 28, 2017   💬 116   🔁 1,578   ♡ 3,811

Tea Pain was just funnin' ya. Of course he didn't. It was all that danged Obama's fault! Even though Obama fired Flynn in 2014 for a number of personality and credibility issues, Trump claimed it was Obama that failed to "properly vet him." It wasn't Trump's responsibility to vet the man that would head his National Security Council, it was Obama's. Let this silliness sink in. Trump, the "birther-in-chief," claimed Obama perpetuated the "greatest fraud in election history," but yet asked us to believe he blindly trusted an "illegitimate president" with a forged birth certificate to "vet" his National Security Chief. Don't that take the rag off the bush?

Tea Pain
@TeaPainUSA

It's political karma that after Trump's 8 years claimin' Obama was illegitimate, he winds up as the 1st President elected by Russia.

11:24 AM - Jan 7, 2017   💬 68   🔁 1,464   ♡ 2,478

Funny thing about karma: it only has to be right once. But with Donald Trump, karma was right every time. It seemed that no matter what stupid thing Trump did, there was a vintage Trump tweet that said the exact opposite. Tea Pain don't know how you like your poetic justice, but he likes his deep-fried, then slathered in butter!

You couldn't write a better plot twist than the one Trump wrote for himself. For five years, he whipped up the racists, white supremacists, neo-Nazis and other garden-variety peckerwoods into a white-hot frenzy, claimin' that Barack Obama was an "illegitimate president" who was secretly colludin' with the Muslims and Iran. More than once Trump alluded that Obama was a "secret Muslim" and the "founder of ISIS."

He ruthlessly manufactured or forwarded one nutball fake-news story after another about Hillary Clinton secretly sellin' out America to Russia or runnin' a pedophile ring from the basement of a D.C. pizzeria.

The truth has a way of catchin' up with all of us, and Tea'll be danged if the truth didn't throw a lasso around ol' Donald Trump and tie him to the tracks of an on-comin' train! After Mr. Obama and Mrs. Hillary put up with all his hateful shenanigans, it was only right and just that Trump is accomplishin' nothin' while bein' swallered up in a growin' cloud of scandal.

- - -

Donald Trump is Comin' to Town

He's making a list, he's checking it twice
He's gonna keep track who's Muslim or White

Donald Trump is comin' to town

He knows if you're a Muslim
He knows if you are black
But hide if you're a Mexican
Cause he wants to send you back

If you're name is Ahmed, you better not pray
He'll shut down your mosque and ship you away

Donald Trump is comin' to town
Donald Trump is comin'...to town

11. LET TRUMP BEAT TRUMP

Tea Pain
@TeaPainUSA

This is the kind of presidency you get when you put a largemouth bass in charge of a bait shop.

7:54 PM - Aug 8, 2017   💬 124   ♻ 1,013   ♡ 3,527

Tea Pain will be the first to admit he didn't see Donald Trump comin'. As a matter of fact, Tea Pain discounted him at every turn, probably because Tea Pain loves America so much he never dreamed there would be so many silly folks that would vote for him. Tea Pain ain't wrong often, but in this case he was wrong and wrong "bigly."

Trump sold America on the idea of runnin' the country like a business; more accurately, his business. Trump likes to tell the story that he started with a *small* million dollar loan from his daddy and turned it into a vast empire. Turns out that "empire" might be only "half-vast" at best.

Trump did start with a loan, but still inherited most of his wealth from Daddy Fred. Currently, Trump is estimated to be worth about four billion, but the Associated Press did the math and found that if Trump had just invested his inheritance into common index funds, his current wealth would be over 13 billion. For all of

Trump's alleged business acumen, he couldn't even outperform the average American's 401K plan.

So, yes America, he's runnin' the country just like it's one of his businesses… and that's the problem.

Tea Pain
@TeaPainUSA

When Donald Trump gets stressed he does his own laundry. He says separating whites from colors relaxes him. @realDonaldTrump

9:02 PM - Jun 30, 2016   ♡ 30   ↻ 647   ♡ 973

The hardest pill for most Americans to swaller was comin' to terms with the fact that racism and bigotry was way more prevalent in America than we ever dreamed. Even though Tea Pain was in the Tea Party back in 2008, he was still proud when America elected its first African-American president. Was it naive of Tea to think we'd turned the corner on hate and finally put racism in our rear view mirror?

Turns out, a black president was too much for some folks to handle, and they quickly found a home in the Tea Party, which was the de-evolution of American politics that gave birth to the birther-in-chief, Donald Trump.

Tea Pain
@TeaPainUSA

3 groups voted for Trump.

1. Racists
2. Folks that don't have a problem with racism.
3. Fools that don't believe the first 2 groups exist.

9:11 AM - Nov 16, 2016

💬 162   🔁 2,302   ♡ 3,460

Tea Pain ain't sayin' that all Trumpers are racists or that all racists are Trumpers, but Tea Pain is sayin' that Trumpers certainly don't have any problems with other Trumpers bein' racists.

Tea Pain
@TeaPainUSA

When Trump says John McCain "eboldens the enemy", does he mean ISIS or the New York Times?

8:53 AM - Feb 9, 2017

💬 106   🔁 1,272   ♡ 3,506

As of July 1st, 2017, out of approximately 770 tweets Trump sent as president, 85 were attacks on the media, 67 tweets focused on jobs, and about 27 concerned the U.S. military. ISIS, who Trump calls the "greatest threat to our national security," didn't even crack his top three topics.

Tea Pain
@TeaPainUSA

Trump is not some master tactician or even a mad genius .
He's proof Democracy was not designed to be run by an 8
year old.

10:55 AM - Jul 2, 2017

💬 263   ↻ 2,883   ♡ 7,799

Trump totally bamboozled the press, not by bein' smarter than
them or more clever. He fooled 'em because they had never
covered a president with the emotional maturity of an 8 year old
before. The media tried their best to report on Trump as if he was
a "normal" candidate, but it ended up makin' them look crazier
than a bobcat at a county fair.

It was almost sport watchin' them talkin' heads tryin' to explain
that Trump's most recent 3 a.m. tweetstorm was actually a
masterful distraction from more jobs bein' sent overseas or another
white nationalist shootin', when all it was was an outta control
man-baby havin' a hissy fit cause a reporter didn't shower him with
the appropriate amount of praise. For the record, "praise" is the
second most favorite thing Trump likes to be showered with.

Tea Pain
@TeaPainUSA

Trump says he can release the most classified data anytime
he chooses, but can't release his tax returns due to an
"audit."

12:31 PM - May 16, 2017

💬 518   ↻ 14,368   ♡ 23,270

On any given day, Trump is slippier than WD-40, but when it came
to his tax returns, he was straight-up KY Jelly. Ol' Teflon Don
made promise after promise to release his tax returns, but he never

did, and his folks never cared. Funny thing, a lotta his followers on Twitter actually said they *don't even wanna see his tax returns*. Folks, when it comes to political intrigue, Trump's tax returns is the Holy Grail... the political equivalent of seein' Angelina Jolie and Brad Pitt sunbathin' in the nude. If somebody told you they didn't wanna see that, they just ain't hooked up right.

Trump's followers, as well as the entire GOP, shielded him at every turn to keep him from havin' to release them. Can you imagine standin' behind a candidate 100% while knowin' full well his tax returns would reveal a dozen dirty dealings with the same "evil empire" Ronald Reagan warned us about?

The real kicker was the day Trump hosted the Russian ambassador and the Russian foreign minister in the Oval Office. He banned the U.S. press, but allowed the Russians to snap pictures of him bowin' and scrapin' to his new overlords. Trump really wanted to ingratiate himself to Putin's lackeys, so he dished some juicy gossip fresh from Israeli intelligence.

The press made a big stink of a U.S. president betrayin' America's closest ally in the Middle East, but Trump's inner circle assured us the president can "declassify" any intelligence at any time. This, unfortunately, is the same staff that assured us Trump remains mysteriously powerless to release his tax returns because they've been "under audit" since Hitler was a corporal. Trump's diehard band of logic-proof lackeys lapped up this blatant contradiction like sauce on a slab of ribs, provin' the old sayin': "None of us is as stupid as all of us."

Tea Pain
@TeaPainUSA

FUN FACT: The only folks in D.C. that claim Russia didn't hack our election are the ones under investigation for colludin' with 'em.

3:35 PM - Jun 21, 2017

💬 294　↻ 8,451　♡ 17,663

All 17 U.S. intelligence agencies unanimously and unambiguously concurred that Russia meddled in the 2016 election, and everyone in D.C agreed with the sole exception, of course, of Donald Trump. Trump's like the feller whose previous 16 girlfriends all caught him with another woman. When his current girlfriend catches him in the act, he claims the other woman is a plant hired by CNN and all 17 girls are hormonal, unstable and part of a massive #fakenews conspiracy. Come to think of it, Trump treats the FBI, CIA and NSA just like he's treated every woman he's ever known.

Tea Pain
@TeaPainUSA

Trump ran for President to "pay back the country that helped him so much." The FBI's workin' 24/7 to figure out which country that is.

10:24 AM - Apr 5, 2017

💬 250　↻ 6,645　♡ 13,068

Brock Throckmorton was the richest feller in Gizzard Ridge. He inherited a lot of money when his folks passed. He's got a sweet 2009 Ford F-150 and the biggest double wide they make. Despite all these blessings, he is easily the angriest man in all of Fartlett county. If you looked up the word "rude" in the dictionary, Brock's picture would be right there beside it. Tea Pain believes it was because Brock's daddy didn't hug him enough.

Brock is currently on wife number four, and he's always got his eye on a newer, younger model to trade the current Mrs. Throckmorton in on. This ol' scudder has a menagerie of self-destructive habits, but his most well-known is his love for the ponies down in Hot Springs. Every weekend during race season, ol' Throckmorton is down at Oaklawn doin' his best to burn through his inheritance. Apparently he still had money left over, so he started bettin' year-round through off-track gamin'. Skeeter Johnson, Gizzard Ridge's most connected individual and "guy who knows a guy," handles all of Brock's "equestrian investments." The rest of us just call Skeeter what he really is: a bookie.

Funny thing: when Brock would come into the Skid Mark every day about 4:30, he'd always have some story about some feller he slickered into doin' work for him, only to refuse to pay him because of some tiny flaw Brock would find. To hear Brock tell it, everybody was out to cheat *him* outta something. Long story short, Brock had nothin' good to say about anybody except himself. Then the oddest thing happened.

Word got around Gizzard Ridge that Brock had managed to get upside down big-time with ol' Skeeter over a bet on a horse out in California. Brock woke up on the mornin' of July 7th at 7:00 a.m. It just so happened that in the seventh race at Santa Anita that day, there were seven horses, so Brock wagered seven thousand dollars on the number seven horse... who was coincidentally named Seventh Son. The only flaw in the plan? The horse came in seventh. Rumor has it Skeeter worked out a progressive installment plan for Brock to pay back the debt that was tilted greatly in Skeeter's favor.

While payin' back the loss, whenever Brock was holdin' court at the Skid Mark and ol' Skeeter would come in, Brock would set up straight and treat Skeeter like he was the queen of England. Brock always laughed way too loud at Skeeter's jokes and addressed him with "yes sir" and "no sir."

Skeeter couldn't help but take advantage of this situation by makin' some pretty rough digs at Brock, like sayin' he sleeps with Brock's wife when he's outta town and how Brock's butt keeps gettin' bigger every day and stuff. All Brock could do was sit there smilin' like nothing was wrong, while the giant pulsin' vein in his forehead begged to differ.

Tea Pain's Twitter buddy, Malcolm Nance, has a funny sayin' that's mighty appropriate here and relevant to Trump's apparent allegiance to Russia: "A gambler never insults his bookie."

Tea Pain
@TeaPainUSA

The North Korea situation is mighty dicey. You can't predict how a maniacal cult leader with a huge army will react. Or Kim Jong Un either.

11:23 AM - Apr 13, 2017

441   10,863   20,824

Have you noticed when Kim Jong Un puts journalists in jail, Republicans call him a "dictator," but when Trump calls the press the "enemy of the people," the same folks call him a "genuine leader in touch with the common man"?

Or when Kim Jong Un launches a new missile, he's a "maniacal warmonger," but when Trump fires 59 cruise missiles into Syria, he's a "powerful, decisive leader"?

The funny thing is, these two "leaders" is more alike than different. They inherited everything they own from their daddies. They both love to threaten nuclear war. They both despise a free press. Neither are physically fit, and they both have four dollar haircuts, so why the big difference? Easy. One is Asian. The other's Caucasian.

Tea Pain
@TeaPainUSA

Trump wants us to believe Obama tapped his phones, but forgot to leak his tax returns. #TrumpRussia

5:55 PM - Mar 5, 2017

💬 142   ↺ 4,052   ♡ 7,611

When news started leakin' out that Trump's crew had been chatty with Russian intelligence operatives, Trump did what he does best: blamed his problems on black folks. Accordin' to Trump, the only crime that transpired was that Obama "tapped" his phones and Susan Rice had unmasked his campaign staff. The fact he'd committed treason with America's number one adversary was irrelevant; the true tragedy is how Trump got caught. Trump's followers screamed for "evidence" of collusion for months but believed Trump's accusations without a single shred of it. Obama had already been declared guilty in the court of Trump-inion by virtue of him "presidentin' while bein' black."

Trump never cared to explain why Obama "tapped" his phones yet kept all the information top secret until after he was elected.

Tea Pain
@TeaPainUSA

Tonight a crazy feller drove up the White House and claimed he had a bomb. We know he's crazy cause he thinks Trump works weekends.

1:03 AM - Mar 19, 2017

💬 300   ↺ 5,346   ♡ 12,009

One thing that drove the Tea Party to the verge of bloody revolution was when President Obama went golfin' or took a day off. Even though Obama took half the vacation days of Ronald Reagan or George W. Bush, the Tea Party complained about the wasteful spendin' of the first family. Then came Donald Trump, who made golf and vacations "presidential" again.

Tea Pain
@TeaPainUSA

In 6 weeks, Trump spent more travel budget than Obama did in a year. His supporters are ok with it since they discovered Trump isn't black.

10:38 AM - Mar 3, 2017

💬 218   🔁 5,225   ♡ 8,217

As a matter of fact, during Trump's first six months in office, he played *three times* as much golf as Obama. On top of that, Trump plays golf at Mar-a-lago, Florida, which involves the use of Air Force One and his expensive secret service crew. Trump is on schedule to spend as much on his vacation budget in one year as Obama did in *eight years!* Practicin' true golf-crowd etiquette, the Tea Party remained totally silent as Trump fought ISIS one hole at a time.

Just so happens the Secret Service recently announced they would be "bankrupt" as of September 2017. Trump already burned through their budget with his elaborate golfin' trips and weekly junkets to Trump properties. If Obama had done anything even remotely close to this, the Republicans would have made him a free tar and feather leisure suit.

Tea Pain
@TeaPainUSA

Have you noticed that Conservatives don't call Liberals "Communists" anymore? Must be outta respect for their new mother country.

1:43 PM - Jun 13, 2017

💬 345   🔁 5,025   ♡ 12,398

Tea Pain will be the first to give Trump credit. Nobody builds a more loyal cult than he does. He managed to take the Tea Party and overnight make them stop carin' about the Constitution. He took the party of Reagan, who famously spoke out against Russia as the "Evil Empire," and made them fall in love with a bonafide dictator, Vladimir Putin. Currently 54% of the Republican party has a favorable impression of the Russian dictator, which, coincidentally, is the same percentage of Republicans that think a college education is a "bad thing."

Tea Pain
@TeaPainUSA

The Trump White House is just like "The Bachelorette." Every week he sends a different guy home.

10:28 PM - Jul 28, 2017

💬 347   🔁 2,622   ♡ 8,024

Two houses down the road from Tea Pain's house was ol' man Crumpler's place. Crumpler was in his early fifties, but he had the distinction of bein' married eight times and was workin' on the ninth. Funny thing, he divorced every single one of 'em because they all "falsely" accused him of runnin' around on 'em. Even though over the years, folks around town saw him drivin' around with number six while he was still hitched to number five.

Tea Pain once asked Mr. Crumpler why he'd been married so many times. Without blinkin' an eye, Crumpler shot back, "Cause I can't find a woman worth keepin'."

Tea Pain politely took him at his word, but between you, Tea Pain and the lamp post, Tea suspects the problem lay elsewhere.

Sounds just like ol' Donald Trump, don't it? Trump can't get nothin' done because he can't stop shootin' off his big mouth or stay off Twitter insultin' folks. Seems like every Friday since Trump was elected there's been a rose ceremony where Trump sends another staffer home in tears. Flynn, Epstein, Walsh, Spicer, Priebus, Scaramucci and, most recently, Steve Bannon have been sent to that nice big farm up in country. And every week the press naively suggests that the latest firin' might put the White House back on track.

All in all, 13 major staffers have bit the dirt, but Trump stumbles on, refusin' to own up to his own failures. It's rumored Trump has a sign on his desk that says, "The buck is missing. Someone took it. I blame Obama."

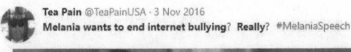

Tea Pain @TeaPainUSA · 3 Nov 2016
Melania wants to end internet bullying? Really? #MelaniaSpeech

"The tweets are coming from inside the house!"

The only way this irony could be more delicious is if it was double-battered, chicken-fried then topped with cream gravy. Just think, if Trump had lost we might have had Callista Gingrich's "Marital Fidelity Foundation," Mary Pat Christie's "Council for Nutrition and Fitness" or the Heidi Cruz "Non-Nasal Communication Initiative."

Tea Pain
@TeaPainUSA

Trump shoots three security guards in the capital rotunda...

Paul Ryan: "It's his first day with a gun. He'll get better over time."

3:46 PM - Jun 8, 2017   190   3,505   8,513

It could be reasonably argued that the first six months of Trump's presidency made the Hindenburg incident look like a fender bender. When pressed about Trump's total lack of competence for the job, House Speaker Paul Ryan brushed it off sayin', "He's just new to this... he'll get better."

Perhaps just to spite Ryan, Trump then threatened to fire special prosecutor Bob Mueller, wage nuclear war on North Korea and invade Venezuela, then publicly supported Nazis and white supremacists.

Note to Paul Ryan: He didn't get better.

Tea Pain
@TeaPainUSA

New poll says 76% of Americans don't trust what Trump says. The other 24% were away attendin' school at Trump University. @realDonaldTrump

10:44 PM - Aug 8, 2017   ◯ 244   ⇄ 4,191   ♡ 12,115

Coincidentally, that 24% also said they would definitely stick a butter knife in an electric socket again.

Tea Pain
@TeaPainUSA

Pastor Jeffress says God gave Trump "authority" to nuke Kim Jong Un. Hope the 25 million other North Koreans don't mind.

9:53 AM - Aug 10, 2017   ◯ 402   ⇄ 1,173   ♡ 3,306

Poor Melania and her campaign to stop cyber bullyin'. In one tweet her husband threatened to bring the force of a thousand suns down on 25 million North Koreans. Not tryin' to say that Trump has a God complex, but 25 million is approximately the number of folks God killed in the Old Testament. Coincidence?

Tea Pain
@TeaPainUSA

Trump: "I want to thank Putin for repossessing Alaska, we're gonna save a bundle on American flags with only 49 stars!"

8:06 PM - Aug 10, 2017

◯ 317   ⇄ 3,731   ♡ 10,246

You really gotta wonder what juicy Kompromat ol' Vladimir is holdin' over Trump's corn-silk coiffure. In retaliation for the Congressional sanctions bill Trump was forced to sign against Russia, Putin kicked 755 foreign diplomats and their staff outta his country. Trump responded, "I want to thank him because we're trying to cut down on payroll."

This saved Trump a lot of money as well. Now he won't have to go to a high-end Nevada brothel and order the "Deluxe Russian Dominatrix Package."

Tea Pain
@TeaPainUSA

Aren't you folks grateful we didn't elect Hillary? We'd have dozens of scandals, criminal investigations and on the brink of nuclear war.

9:10 PM - Aug 11, 2017   💬 198   🔁 1,036   ♡ 2,955

Karma is a beautiful thing. The more Trump talks, the harder it bites. Let's take a quick look at some of Trump's greatest hits.

November 2 in Miami, FL

"If Hillary Clinton were to be elected, it would create an unprecedented and protracted constitutional crisis. Haven't we just been through a lot with the Clintons, right?"

November 2 in Orlando, FL

"Hillary is likely to be under investigation for many years, probably concluding in a criminal trial."

November 4 in Atkinson, NH

"She'll be under investigation for years. She'll be with trials. Our country, we have to get back to work."

November 4 in Wilmington, OH

> "Hillary has engaged in a criminal massive enterprise and cover-ups like probably nobody ever before."

The day Donald Trump put his hand on the Bible and took the oath of office, he became the first American president inaugurated while under FBI criminal investigation. Eight months into his presidency, the traditional honeymoon period, he's starin' down a 33% approval ratin' while support for his impeachment is at 54%. After Trump fired FBI director James Comey because of the growin' Russian collusion investigation, constitutional experts proclaimed that we are on the edge of a "protracted constitutional crisis."

Now that Bob Mueller has been named as the special prosecutor, Trump will "be under investigation for many years, probably concluding in a criminal trial."

As of this writin', Trump was proposin' nuclear war against North Korea, a military ground incursion into Venezuela and spendin' another generation in Afghanistan.

"But, but, her emails!"

Tea Pain
@TeaPainUSA

Ain't it sad when two Nazis leave the White House and there's still more to go? @realDonaldTrump

8:47 PM - Aug 25, 2017   🗨 143   ↻ 2,248   ♡ 6,299

Tea Pain's proud to say as of the writin' of this book, two-thirds of Trump's unholy Nazi Trinity are gone from the White House.

Steve Bannon was given his pink slip right after the Charlottesville debacle. He landed softly in his old Nazi nest the next day runnin'

Hatebart News. The good thing about Steve is you don't have to worry about him turnin' to alcohol.

While Hurricane Harvey slammed the Texas coast, news came out that Sebastian Gorka was let go from his "job" as White House counter-terrorism advisor. This ol' goose-stepper was actually silly enough to wear his prized Nazi medal to one of Trump's inaugural balls. Sadly, Trump lacked the inaugural balls to fire his Nazi pal and had to hire General Kelly to do it. This proves Trump's no racist, because as soon as he found out about Gorka's Nazi past, he jumped right on it and got him outta the White House in less than 8 months.

That leaves Joseph Goebbels's lovechild and senior policy advisor Stephen Miller, who just last week went on national television and proclaimed the beautiful poem on the base of the Statue of Liberty was "irrelevant" because it was "added later" and not applicable to American policy. Miller essentially nixed the "give me your tired, your poor, your huddled masses" in favor of an Anglo-Saxon-centric merit-based immigration policy. Immigrants will receive bonus points for speakin' English and havin' a high-paid job offer waitin' on them in the U.S. Miller sees Lady Liberty's torch not as a light, but as a flame-thrower to turn back the wave of dirty immigrants that want to come here and kill us all.

Tea Pain
@TeaPainUSA

It would be a far simpler investigation if we just search for members of the Trump administration with ties to America. #TrumpRussia

1:02 AM - Feb 28, 2017   💬 165   🔁 3,477   ♡ 6,710

On a number of occasions, Trump assured us his campaign had "zero contact" with Russia, even after his campaign manager, Paul Manafort, stepped down for ties to Russia. His spokespeople went on TV and said Manafort was an "unpaid volunteer" that had "minimum interaction with the campaign for a very short time."

Turns out, you couldn't swing a dead cat in Trump Tower without hittin' a POP (Pal of Putin).

One after another of Trump's team was caught with their hands in Vlad's cookie jar: Carter Page, Roger Stone, even Trump's own son-in-law and boy wunderkind Jared Kushner.

When Trump's National Security Advisor, Mike Flynn, was fired for gettin' caught talkin' to the Russian ambassador, Kellyanne Conjob made the rounds on TV and assured us again that Flynn only played a "minor role" in the Trump cosmos. As is the norm in Trump-World, the truth is just the opposite. Considerin' the totality of Trump's foreign policy bona fides was "Taco Bowl Tuesday" at Trump Tower, Mike Flynn had to be workin' harder than a one-legged waitress at IHOP.

Donald J. Trump ● @realDonaldTrump · Jun 26
The real story is that President Obama did NOTHING after being informed in August about Russian meddling. With 4 months looking at Russia...
...and did not want to "rock the boat." He didn't "choke," he colluded or obstructed, and it did the Dems and Crooked Hillary no good.

If y'all remember, Trump denied that Russia hacked our election for close to a year; that is, until he found the opportunity to blame it on Obama. Right about the time the intelligence community published proof that Putin himself had sent the order for the election to be hacked in favor of Trump over Hillary, Trump did a 180 and blamed it on Obama for "doin' nothin'," because, you know, that's what black folks do.

Tea Pain
@TeaPainUSA

Trump is havin' his "It's not my fault I'm a traitor, Obama should have stopped me" moment.

9:27 PM - Jun 23, 2017   ◯ 451   ⟲ 8,289   ♡ 19,915

Nobody ever accused Trump supporters of bein' what scientists call "critical thinkers." Accordin' to Trump's latest version of the truth, Russia hacked the election, and Obama did nothin' to stop 'em. Ol' Donnie doubled down on delusion, goin' so far as to claim Obama himself secretly "colluded" with Russia so Trump would get elected!

Gettin' Trump elected was only part of Obama's dastardly clever plan. Obama and the intel agencies would then fabricate evidence to make it appear Trump had colluded so he would be impeached, all to avenge Hillary!

Now a sane and sober feller would ask: "Wouldn't it be easier for Obama to fake the evidence first and just let Hillary win?" Sure that would be the easy way, but that's not how sinister multinational cabals work.

Ain't it funny that what reasonable folks see as total foolishness, Trump's supporters see as 22-dimensional chess?

Tea Pain
@TeaPainUSA

When you pardon racists, you surrender the moral authority to call for Americans to "come together and move on." @realDonaldTrump

11:18 PM - Aug 25, 2017   ⬭ 232   ⬮ 3,976   ♡ 8,696

Trump unleashed another storm of controversy durin' an actual storm. While all the nation was fixated on the devastatin' effects of Hurricane Harvey, Trump was settin' about doin' the dirty deeds despots do under the cover of night and tempest. He announced he was pardonin' Sheriff Joe Arpaio, his confidant in his little "Band of Birthers."

This came during the same week Trump called for America to accept and love one another.

When a scoundrel like Trump defends neo-Nazis, white supremacists and the KKK, then asks us to "come together and move on," we need to see what he's really sayin'. This is a psychological technique to project the focus from the guilty to those who cast judgement on them. Trump's essentially tellin' mainstream America if you don't accept these deplorable racists, the problem is *you*, not them. Loving and acceptin' each other is a good thing, right? So why aren't you willing' to do it? This is nothin' short of normalizin' racism in America.

Tea Pain
@TeaPainUSA

When Trump defends racism and pardons a racist, then says we should accept & love one another, he means we should accept & love racism.

8:56 AM - Aug 26, 2017   ⬭ 128   ⬮ 921   ♡ 2,441

Tea Pain is just like you - saddened to see this level of acceptance of racism and bigotry by a surprisingly large part of our nation.

America has already defeated this ideology twice, once at Appomattox and again at the Battle of the Bulge. Looks like the white supremacists are gettin' ready to learn that lesson the hard way one more time.

Tea Pain
@TeaPainUSA

Trump blames McConnell for not "protecting" him from Russia probes. You know what should be the best "protection"? Innocence.

5:06 PM - Aug 22, 2017   ○ 418   ↻ 5,902   ♡ 15,566

Trump is the most guilty actin' "innocent" man Tea Pain's ever seen. After callin' the Trump-Russia scandal a "hoax" more times than we can count, Trump called key members of Congress and the intelligence community and asked them to quash the Congressional investigations and/or publicly claim his innocence. He then met several times with FBI director James Comey, askin' him to go easy on Mike Flynn and encouragin' him to stop the FBI criminal investigation.

After Comey refused to make a personal oath of loyalty to Trump himself, Trump fired him and told NBC news he did it because of the Russia investigation.

Then it came out that Trump got crossways with Senate Majority Leader Mitch McConnell, because the "Turtle" wouldn't protect the "Hair" in the Russia probes.

A fox caught stealin' one of your chickens will do the honest thing and run. But Trump's the kind of fox that blames the guard dogs for lettin' him get into the yard, the farmer for not properly securing the hen house and the chickens for bein' delicious in the first place. Trump-fox then accuses the farmer, guard dogs, chickens and CNN of participatin' in an elaborate barnyard conspiracy to frame him for the farmer's fondness of fried chicken.

Turns out Trump-fox was the true hero, tryin' to save the chickens, one at a time.

Tea Pain
@TeaPainUSA

Trump has a severe speech impediment. He can't say "White Supremacy", "Neo-Nazi", "KKK" or "Domestic Terrorism."

3:00 PM - Aug 12, 2017

💬 309   ↻ 2,841   ♡ 5,732

Karma bit Trump hard in the hiney on this one. Addressing the nation after the Charlottesville terrorist attack, Trump refused to call the murderer out for what he was: a domestic terrorist. Instead he blamed the victim's compatriots as bein' responsible for the hate as well. There's one thing we've learned about a Trump presidency: there is always a tweet for everything.

Donald J. Trump ✔ @realDonaldTrump · 12 Jun 2016
Is President Obama going to finally mention the words **radical Islamic terrorism**? If he doesn't he should immediately resign in disgrace!

Donald Trump rightfully deserves every bad thing that has come his way. It's truly poetic justice that each and every scandal is that of his own makin'. The heart of Trump's campaign was built on nothin' more than destroyin' Obama's presidential legacy over what appears to be a distaste for his skin color and a childish jealousy fueled by Obama's abundant talent and sound character. When you stack Donald Trump up against Barack Obama, two words stand out to describe Trump's philosophy and agenda: *small and petty*.

Tea Pain
@TeaPainUSA

Tea Pain would call Donald Trump small and petty, but that would be offensive to small and petty people everywhere. #TrumpRallyPhoenix

10:29 PM - Aug 22, 2017   49   447   1,902

Tea Pain's gonna go out on a limb and make a prediction. As Bob Mueller's investigation goes deeper into Trump's finances, chances are good he will find some prison-worthy naughtiness by the Trump crime family. Tea Pain predicts Trump will try to cut some deal where he will resign in exchange for the charges bein' dropped. He will then claim he fulfilled his promise to "Make America Great Again" and try to spin his resignation as a victory on his terms. In essence: a reality-show endin' for the reality-show president.

So… much… winnin'.

- - -

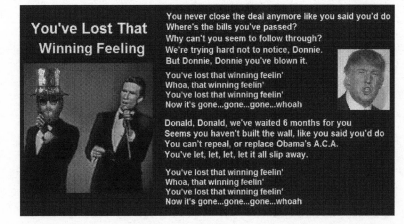

12. TEN COMMANDMENTS OF TWEETIN'

Tea Pain's been called "Twitter's premier troll-buster," and while Tea Pain appreciates the honor, it's really nothin' special. Anybody can do it if you just foller a simple set of rules. Think of it as the "Ten Commandments of Tweetin." Tea Pain will sharpen your Twitter game with this simple set of dos and don'ts.

1. First, Do No Harm

Erik here is a prime example of what happens when you violate the Twit-o-cratic oath: "First, do no harm." Ol' Erik never met a death threat he didn't like. This scamp has been suspended at least a dozen times as of last count and has been the source of a whole lotta Liberal laughter!

Erik is another one of them naive Trumpers that hated Obama for gettin' him healthcare, then voted for Trump so he could take it away. He's obviously a proud feller that is willin' to die for the white reason.

If you're ever in doubt about how your own Twitter career is comin' along, here's a good piece of advice. Stop and ask yourself: "Am I better off than I was 3 tweets ago?"

If you answered "No," chances are, you're Erik. And by the way, ladies, he's "singel!"

2. Never Misspell an Insult

This is the social media equivalent of pullin' the pin on a grenade and tossin' the pin instead. Before you let loose a scathin' retort about the other feller's belief system, you best check your spellin' and grammar twice, or you'll wind up like this poor feller:

L-DeplorableHarrison @p8triat   Mar 22, 2015
Replying to @Centinel1787
. @Centinel1787 Trailer Trash > @teapainusa < #Athiest - assumes IT knows BILBLE

Tea Pain
@TeaPainUSA

@p8triat Brother, that woulda landed a lot harder if you had spelled "Bible" and "Atheist" right!

L-DeplorableHarrison
@p8triat

dahhhhhhhhhh @clydetheslyde separation of church and
state r not in constitution, Moran

9:22 PM - Jun 30, 2014

Those little red lines in your spellchecker are workin' hard to keep
you from lookin' like an idiot. Don't let the air outta your own
balloon; listen to 'em!

Tea Pain @TeaPainUSA · 11 Oct 2015
This is what happens when a Tea Party gun nut starts thinkin'.
@homebuilderpa #2A

2A Supporter @homebuilderpa · 34s
@TeaPainUSA @DeadlyRBF @RoryBBellows1 @SeanC75
Wow. Just when I though you couldn't get any stupider...

9:29 PM - 11 Oct 2015 · Details

The First Amendment protects your right to act a fool on Twitter,
but the Second Amendment can't protect you from shootin'
yourself in the foot.

3. Don't Let Your Own Words Bite You

Donald J. Trump ✓
@realDonaldTrump

An 'extremely credible source' has called my office and told me that @BarackObama's birth certificate is a fraud.

3:23 PM - Aug 6, 2012

Donald J. Trump ✓
@realDonaldTrump

Anytime you see a story about me or my campaign saying "sources said," DO NOT believe it. There are no sources, they are just made up lies!

2:20 AM - Sep 30, 2016

Once Trump began runnin' for president and folks started studyin' his Twitter feed, it was discovered you could find a tweet he made a couple years ago that would flatly contradict something he tweeted today. That's really nothin' new, folks, cause fools have been doin' that for thousands of years. It only took modern technology and social media to trick 'em into puttin' it into writing.

kiki biscane @kikibiscane · 23 Jun 2016
how do you sit in church and Goddamn America?

Tea Pain @TeaPainUSA · 23 Jun 2016
Reckon the same way you go to church and say this...

kiki biscane @kikibiscane · 3h
Mother fuckers on Twitter ain't Shit

Put this into practice for yourself. If somebody is callin' you or your team "racist," search his Twitter feed. You'll almost always find the n-word or other unsavory nicknames for minorities and such. If someone calls you stupid for makin' a typo, give his feed a quick once-over, and you'll find he does to English what Brutus did to Caesar.

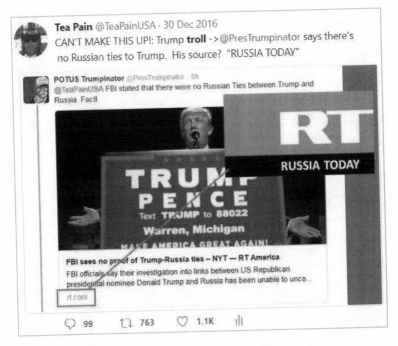

Pro-tip: Don't use Russia Today to prove your candidate has no ties to Russia.

4. Think Before You Tweet

You shouldn't even have to tell folks this, but even Tea Pain is still surprised by the lack of thought that goes into some of these trolls' silly tweets. Take ol' Wild Bill here for example. Bill was no doubt proud when he let this one fly. He was sho nuff excited to be only the 14 millionth troll on Twitter to bust out this 150-year-old debunked talkin' point:.

WildBillforAmerica @WildBillusa   Jun 15, 2015
Democrats want their KKK back! RETWEET

Tea Pain
@TeaPainUSA

@WildBillusa Who do they want it back FROM, brother Bill? Ooopsies!

Without thinkin', ol' Bill admitted to the whole world that Conservatives are currently in control of the KKK. While we's on the topic of the KKK, here's one of the most effective comebacks Tea Pain's ever found to deal with these silly critters and their KKK foolishness.

Dinesh D'Souza ✓
@DineshDSouza

.@PJMedia_com Did Hillary forget to mention last night the Democrats were the party of the Ku Klux Klan?

Tea Pain
@TeaPainUSA

Tea Pain welcomes @DineshDSouza to walk into any KKK meetin' and accuse them ol' boys of bein' an Obama voter.
3:31 PM - Jul 29, 2016

💬 94   🔁 236   ♡ 393

This one always stops 'em in their tracks. Tea Pain's had over two dozen trolls block and run after gettin' this tasty riff served up in their timeline. Can you imagine these silly trolls actually think that a buncha Liberal Democrats run the most infamous racist organization in American history, while simultaneously campaignin' for the first African-American president? If these folks were any slower you'd have to water 'em twice a week.

Dev Waldron
@Dev_Waldron

We've had a Black president for 8 years now. I think the whole "racism" thing is done.
10:12 AM - Jun 19, 2016

Poor Dev. He stopped to think once and never got started back up again. Fortunately for ol' Dev, Trump loves the "poorly educated."

5. Thou Shalt Not Project Onto Others

Cloyd Rivers
@CloydRivers

Hey Hillary voters, Santa has seen your posts this year. Y'all are gettin' a copy of the Constitution & a dictionary for Christmas. Merica.

Tea Pain
@TeaPainUSA

Because Conservatives are notorious for re-gifting things they never use.

First, let it be said that Tea Pain thinks Brother Cloyd is a fine feller that loves America. As a matter of fact, when Tea Pain was just gettin' started on Twitter, folks used to compare Tea Pain to Brother Cloyd. They'd say things like "Tea Pain reminds me of Cloyd Rivers back when he used to be funny," or "Tea Pain's like Cloyd Rivers if Cloyd was witty and clever," and other fun stuff like that. Tea Pain felt mighty honored just to be compared to him.

The big mistake brother Cloyd made with this particular tweet is that he got a might cocky and projected his team's natural weaknesses onto his opponents. Truth be told, the three documents Conservatives consult the least are the Constitution, the Bible and the dictionary. Brother Cloyd lobbed a big ol' fat softball up there, and Tea Pain naturally had to swing for the fences.

6. Thou Shalt Not Pretend to Be a Minority

Tea Pain wishes he had a dollar for every Trump troll he's rolled for pretendin' to be a minority. These folks are the lowest of the low. To enforce the idea that they're "black," they often use phony "ghetto talk" which sounds like a racist's cliché idea of what black folks talk like. When Tea Pain exposed this ol' scoundrel, he switched his bio pic, wrapped himself in the flag and pretended to be a spokesperson for military vets. Ol' Jason here doesn't understand how Google image search works, cause it revealed he stole his original bio picture from the Mingle2 datin' site. Funny how these ol' white racists secretly dream of bein' handsome black fellers.

Tea Pain @TeaPainUSA · 21 Nov 2016
#TrollOfTheDay Meet "Andy" @clintonscam. He's "straight outta Compton" but his photo's "straight outta **Shutterstock**."

Andy Carlson
@clintonscam

Blacks For Trump

Compton, CA

Joined October 2016

Andy Carlson @clintonscam · Nov 17
My Grandfather was a Slave . He was Sold by the Africans. It was not the white mans fault. Blacks need to get over it. #StudyyourHistory

Andy Carlson @clintonscam · Nov 16
#OBAMA Completely sucks. What has he done for African Americans. I think there is more racism the last eight years. It was the White in Him

Andy Carlson @clintonscam · Nov 7
In Compton Most of everyone I talked to wants to go back to work. They are mostly voting for #TrumpPence16 They Do know about #CrookedHilary

One of Tea Pain's favorites is this Trump troll that was so lazy, he didn't even remove the watermark from his Shutterstock bio pic.

Pro-Tip: Anytime you see one of these "minorities for Trump" accounts, check out the bio photo. Learn to use Google image search, and you can bust these fakers in a New York minute!

7. Thou Shalt Not Be a Religious Hypocrite

 Tea Pain @TeaPainUSA · 29 Dec 2015
#TrollOfTheDay This TRUMP "Christian" -> @TSG_Silent prays
to Jesus **with a Judas mouth.** #CussingForChrist

 Jason becker
@TSG_SiLent

 Jason becker @TSG_SiLent · Dec 25
@ComradeEnver @JimJlr2 @neonfeldman @revteapain @duhbearz @ZaffodB
I haven't done meth in about 7 years. I was saved by **Jesus** June 2010.

 Jason becker @TSG_SiLent · Dec 26
@ZaffodB @duhbearz @ComradeEnver @JimJlr2 @revteapain
liberals are fucking pussies might as well take it in the ass feminists.

 Jason becker @TSG_SiLent · Dec 26
@JimJlr2 @ComradeEnver @ZaffodB @duhbearz @revteapain pussy
ass lbgt faggot bitch

 Jason becker @TSG_SiLent · Dec 27
@GeorgeWill burn in hell you fucking faggot. We want trump!

 Jason becker @TSG_SiLent · Dec 26
@revteapain @JimJlr2 @ComradeEnver @ZaffodB @duhbearz death to all
Muslims!!!!

Tea's mama used to say, "You can't pray to Jesus with a Judas
mouth." Mama was right. The Bible's mighty clear about that. "Do
not let any unwholesome talk come out of your mouths." -
Ephesians 4:29. Ol' Jason here musta not got to that part of the
Holy Word yet, even though he got "saved" seven years ago.

Jason's just follerin' in the footsteps of Republican Jesus. In Jason's
mind, he's sure Jesus went up on the mountain and cussed all the
Hillary voters for bein' a bunch of "Libtards." Or his favorite
passage, when Jesus chided the poor for bein' a buncha gubment
teet suckers. Oh, the stories Jason's brain could tell us once
properly medicated!

If Tea Pain's seen it once, he's seen it ten thousand times. Almost every time folks start flingin' their faith around like a battle-axe, sure as shootin' their timeline is full of #CussingForChrist.

Tea Pain @TeaPainUSA · 11 Jan 2016
Meet Dennis, a Trump "Christian" who's comfortable with Hate as well as his obvious Heterosexuality. @GrandestParty

Dennis
@grandestparty

Traditional conservative and founder of Political Policy. My Inspirations are Edmund Burke, John Adams, Russell Kirk and William F. Buckley, Jr.

Dennis @grandestparty · Jan 6
@bobbiejaneV @dhwbsjejjj @Patrick_Fogerty @mcfarlas1947 I'm Christian just Telling the TRUTH about U babykilling Christianphobes

Dennis @grandestparty · Jan 8
@CaffeineAndHate ah another hanes-grazer. We Heteros STILL laugh at you Homos despite all your freakin rainbows. HAHAHA

Dennis @grandestparty · 29 Nov 2015
@GntxD junior homo moron hate-America Christianphobe thinks only military can have guns 😂😂😂-like all little fascists he ignores Constitution

Dennis @grandestparty · 29 Nov 2015
@GntxD The 2nd Amendment IS an individual right you retarded loser hate-America Christianphobe babykilling homo!

Dennis @grandestparty · 10 Oct 2015
@Sethrogen oh btw did I tell you to go fuck yourself today you fat stupid slob?

Dennis @grandestparty · 9 Oct 2015
@Sethrogen fuck u you racist hateful 1 hit wonder.U leftard couldn't carry Dr. @RealBenCarson bags.Ur ideal role would b as KKK Grand Wizard

Don't get Tea Pain started on ol' Dennis here. He's been banned from Twitter more times than Cher had farewell tours. And don't let the fact his bio pic was taken in an airport men's room distract you from the fact that he's 100% heterosexual. As a matter of fact, he's so comfortable with his sexual orientation that he only mentions it in every third tweet.

And is he a Christian? Heck yes! If you don't believe him, he'll cuss you till you do.

8. Don't Call Folks That Beat You Twice "Losers"

Irony has no place in American politics. How many times has a right-wing troll tried to make fun of you by sayin', "At least I didn't vote for that loser, Obama!?"

They say when you point your finger at somebody, you got three fingers pointin' back at you. If there is ever an Irony Hall of Fame, there will be an entire wing dedicated to people that called Barack Obama an "idiot" while declarin' Sarah Palin "a brilliant choice for a running mate."

9. Don't Be a Blatant Racist

Anybody that's spent a few days on Twitter has bumped into ol'
Jack Posobiec. Jack is Doyle from Slingblade, but without all the
redeemin' qualities. Jack must be a really smart feller, cause he said
so himself on Twitter, tellin' all his tweeps he's got an IQ of 151.
You think a "super smart" feller like Jack wouldn't have made such
a silly mistake.

Jack tweeted about an African-American church that had burned in
Mississippi on November 2, 2016. The scoundrels that done it left
a message on the side of the church: "Vote Trump." This looked
mighty bad for the Trump team so, like any good Trump
supporter, Jack went huntin' for a black feller to pin it on. Because
Jack is so smart, he found the culprit in no time. It was a black
feller that was previously arrested in St. Louis for church arson.
Only problem is, he was arrested 3 days before the Mississippi fire
and was in the slammer when it happened.

Now this fact alone would have stopped any honorable person, but
not Jack. He wasn't about to let a tiny detail like the suspect bein'
in jail 500 miles away spoil the opportunity to blame black folks for
this crime. Jack ain't no liberal nancy-pants that sees the world in

157

indecisive shades of grey. He sees things clearly in black and white. Well, more like white and white.

Tea Pain busted ol' Jack for this and he got the horse-laugh from thousands on Twitter, but Jack never retracted the story. Jack's a fella of principle that stands by his guns; his racist, xenophobic guns.

10. Seriously, Don't Be a Blatant Racist

This Trump troll, which Tea Pain dubbed as "Spurry," was the source of a lotta Twitter fun on Tea Pain's timeline. He was Tea Pain's muse for lots of amusin' tweets. Let's have a little fun unpackin' these two beauties, shall we?

First of all, if you truly wanna understand the black experience in America, you need to ask a white supremacist from Texas, cause they're the experts. Turns out black folks were "no more persecuted than any other races." Spurry assures us the folks that had it really tough in America the past 241 years was poor white Christian males. Them poor fellers just couldn't catch a break.

Spurry also reminded us that it was Liberals, not him, that were the real racists, even though all his tweets were branded with the "green frog" adopted by white supremacists in the Trump era.

Accordin' to Spurry, who obviously got his PhD at Trump University, the real slavers in the U.S.A was black folks, even as far back as "the 1600's." Spurry kinda overlooked the fact that the United States was formed in 1776, but racists seldom let facts interfere with a good story.

Tea Pain @TeaPainUSA · 3m
@NelsonForTruth @graspinghard Is Obama the most racist president in American history?

Nelson Taylor @NelsonForTruth · 3m
@TeaPainUSA @graspinghard Yes

Tea Pain @TeaPainUSA · 1m
@NelsonForTruth @graspinghard Even more racist than the 8 Presidents that owned slaves?

Nelson Taylor @NelsonForTruth · 43s
@TeaPainUSA @graspinghard Yes

This has got to be, without a doubt, Tea's favorite troll takedown of all time. He's used it time and time again, and every time the trolls walk right into it.

After 100 years of slavery followed by 150 years of racial oppression and inequality, America finally elected its first African American president. Immediately the Tea Party formed, which just happens to be 99.5% white. Now ask yourself, what are the chances that the first black president elected was declared the "worst president in history" by the Tea Party?

This Tea Party troll, like thousands of others, actually went on Twitter, typed "Obama is the most racist president of them all," and clicked "Tweet" without ever stoppin' to think that nine sittin' U.S. Presidents actually owned slaves. When Tea Pain would ask these ol' scudders to list examples of Obama's "racism," they couldn't name a one. The real problem for the Tea Party seemed to be Obama lacked the proper *presidential complexion*.

Tea Pain @TeaPainUSA · 29 Nov 2016
This Trump Alt-Righty -> @SONICkname clearly says minorities ain't "Americans." That was clearly the white thing to say.

MAllenJ
@SONICkname

@TeaPainUSA You love minorities, eh? Well, they sure appreciate it. But if you see any Americans, you be sure to lend a hand, ok?

Another product of the "Make America Hate Again" movement, ol' Allen here is the walkin' embodiment of all that's wrong with the Alt-Right. "Making America White Again" is a tall task, but he's definitely the *white man* for the job.

Tea Pain @TeaPainUSA · 18 Dec 2016
Tea Pain has challenged @ChrisW1425 to give us specific examples of President Obama's **racism**. You're on the clock! twitter.com/ChrisW1425/sta…

Sorry, that page doesn't exist!
You can search Twitter using the search box below or return to the homepage.

Listen close and Tea Pain will share some wisdom with you. Marcus Aurelius asked "What is it in itself? What is *its nature*?" Tea Pain thinks that what Brother Marcus was drivin' at was how do you describe something in one word?

So Tea Pain's gonna ask a similar question, and the answer is the key to understandin' how to deal with all the hateful trolls on Twitter. The question is this: *"What do all people fear the most?"*

Tea Pain's been preachin' the Gospel all his life, and he's seen a lotta folks get saved. You know what *really* brings 'em down front? It's not to serve their feller man. It's not because they wanna be a better person. It's not even because they feel guilty about their sins. It's because when they die, they believe they will have to stand before their Creator and give an account of their life. (Romans 14:12)

There it is friends! In a single word: accountability.

In the tweet above, Chris accused President Obama of bein' a racist. Rather than wastin' dozens of tweets arguin' back and forth, Tea Pain held Chris accountable before God and man. Folks like Chris make idiotic statements because they never imagine bein' held accountable for 'em. You can imagine Chris's surprise when Tea Pain called him out.

Cockroaches scatter when you turn on the lights, and Chris was no different. Not only did he delete the tweet, there was so many tweeps pingin' him for his silly statement, he deleted his account.

So there ya go friends, now you know what Tea Pain knows. Tea's daddy was a good cook that lived by two rules: One, don't put anything in it you don't like, and, two, don't burn it.

So here's Tea Pain's tweetin' advice boiled down to its essence:

1. Never lose your cool.
2. Don't tweet anything you wouldn't want read back to you in a court of law.

That's it. Happy tweetin'!

13. Americanism (Epilogue)

7 Tenets of "Americanism"

1. We ain't against bigger gub'ment or smaller gub'ment. We're against stupid gub'ment.
2. Just because others may not see things our way doesn't mean they don't love America.
3. A woman's body is hers...period!
4. America is beautiful. Love is beautiful. Marriage is for everyone
5. Guns are for huntin' and protectin'. #NoGunNonsense.
6. All faiths, including those without are welcome.
7. We speak the truth, but with grace and love.

If you made it this far, chances are you love America as much as Tea Pain does. Though times are mighty dark right now, Tea Pain has faith in his country and that his American brothers and sisters will overcome the darkness, just like we always do.

What better time to take stock of our Democracy than when its very existence is bein' challenged? Tea Pain believes that movin' forward, we need to remind ourselves that there is so much more that unites us than divides us, and we are stronger when we are diverse as a people, but bound as one in a common vision for freedom.

This is why Tea Pain created the 7 Tenets of Americanism. These seven simple points encompass the essence of what it is to be an American. Once the forces that currently divide us are put asunder, we must promise to recommit to one another and embrace the true essentials of our American selves.

Though the night is dark and your heart grows weary, you are never alone, because Tea Pain luvs ya!

Made in the USA
Middletown, DE
06 September 2017